Kippers for Breakfast

Kippers for Breakfast

Millie Vigor

The Shetland Times Ltd.
Lerwick
2003

Kippers for Breakfast

ISBN 1 898852 98 7

First published by The Shetland Times Ltd., 2003.

British Library Cataloguing-in-Publication Data
A catalogue record for this book is available from the British Library.

Printed and published by
The Shetland Times Ltd.,
Gremista, Lerwick,
Shetland ZE1 0PX, UK.

CONTENTS

CHAPTER ONE

'Well lass. I think you should have a medal.'

I put down my knife and fork and looked at the man sitting at the next table.

'A medal! What for?' I asked.

I was in the restaurant on the *St. Clair*, P & O's ferry to Shetland.

'For eating those kippers for breakfast,' he said. 'We *never* eat kippers for breakfast, not *ever*.'

Oh help. I had labelled myself a non-Shetland person without even uttering a word. I smiled at him.

'They were lovely though,' I said. 'I did enjoy them.'

Sailing overnight from Aberdeen had been the last leg in a journey from Helston in Cornwall to the Shetland Isles. After being made redundant three years running my husband, Slim, an aircraft engineer, was now working for British Airways at Sumburgh Airport. Along with our eleven-year-old son, Michael, I was moving house to join him, the farthest house move I was ever likely to make, from one end of Great Britain to the other. Thank goodness Slim had got time off and was there to help.

This was not my first journey to the islands. After the initial interview, in which Slim had been successful in being taken on, BA asked us to fly to Shetland for what was supposed to be a second interview. In fact it was probably meant to give us a chance to decide if we were prepared to live there. The journey was made in December when daylight hours were few. It snowed and the landscape appeared to be barren and treeless.

Eddie, one of the engineers at the airport, who had known Slim while they were both in the Royal Navy, took us on a sight seeing trip. We went to Lerwick, walked its paved main street and bought souvenirs in one of its shops. We had tea in a little café. It was full of bearded and booted men whose clothes, damp from the falling snow, steamed visibly.

The café had been decorated with what I presumed were odd lots of papers in differing patterns. The one that fascinated me was a vast area covered with pink cabbage roses. With the rivulets of condensation that ran down the walls it reminded me of a garden in the rain.

When we were back at the airport I asked where we would live. It was 1977 and Shetland was buzzing with activity, fully occupied with the oil boom, the North Sea sprouting exploration platforms almost daily. Due to the influx of oil-related workers lack of accommodation appeared to be the biggest drawback. But, 'I know a place for you,' said Eddie. 'It needs a bit of work, but it's not too far away. I'll take you to have a look at it.'

To say that the property Eddie showed us needed a 'bit of work' was the understatement of the year, if not to say a lifetime. A forlorn ruin, it stood at the end of a mile and a half of rough, potholed track, barred in three places by gates, all closed. I was not impressed.

Built of local stone with small windows, remarkably still intact, its roof was tarred and from outside seemed to be in order. It had been, and still was, two croft houses with the usual outbuildings attached. Front porches jutted out from each house. We opened the door to the one that looked best.

'Be careful where you step,' said Eddie. 'The floors are rotten in places.'

The floors were rotten and looking up at the inside of the roof it was not hard to see why. Pinpricks of light shone like stars through little holes in it and it was not hard to come to the conclusion that rain dripping through was responsible for the state of the floors. The house consisted of two rooms, the traditional but and ben. In the centre were the box beds, still with their curtains, though now hanging in shreds. Whether it was just that we were inside and away from a cold wind or not, the atmosphere was warm and welcoming.

We inspected the second house, smaller than the one we had been in, and found it in a worse state of repair. The outbuildings were not any better.

'You can do it up,' said Eddie.

I was watching Slim's face and knew, when I saw the smile on it, that his pioneering spirit when it came to rescuing neglected properties was getting the better of him.

I made for the door. 'Let's go,' I said.

And now it was spring. I was on the high seas sailing to a new land, a new home, a new life. Was I going to fit in? Was I going to be able to cope? Was it all going to be so terribly different to what I'd left behind? Only time would tell.

I hadn't rolled out of my bunk as early as I'd hoped. I'd wanted to be on deck to watch as Shetland appeared on the horizon but, by the time Slim, Michael and I stepped out into the open the ship was well up along the eastern coast. The coastline we were looking at was rugged. The sea foamed against rocky cliffs. At intervals a scattering of houses denoted the position of a village.

'I can't see any trees,' I said. 'Nothing here to soften outlines. It looks rather stark.'

'You're a long way north of Cornwall, Millie. Somewhere about a thousand miles. Climate's rather different.'

'But it can't be that much different to Scotland and they grow a lot of trees there.'

'And most of them are well inland,' said Slim.

We stayed on deck a while, leaned over the rail and watched as the bow wave creamed and curled alongside until Michael said, 'When are we going to have some breakfast?' So we went and had breakfast and I had kippers. Those same kippers that made it abundantly clear to my fellow passenger that I was not a Shetlander.

The *St. Clair* crawled in through Bressay Sound and came to rest at the dockside at 8 a.m. We collected our dog, a collie x King Charles from the kennels and made our way down to the car deck. Our Volkswagen van was there, stuffed full with all the things we thought we couldn't live without. We climbed in and then, with a little flutter of anticipation on my part, followed the car in front and drove off the ship. From the dockside we drove along the seafront, skirted Lerwick, then, leaving it behind, headed south. It was a clear day after rain, the sun shone and colours were vibrant in the clean air. Shetland had put on her best clothes to greet us.

The road along which we travelled took a tortuous way. It sneaked around hillsides, dipped suddenly into valleys then zig-zagged its way out on the other side. At times it clung tightly to the side of a hill, the ground to our left dropping sheer into the ocean, nothing between us but a very fragile post and wire fence. The waves crashing on the rocks below looked very threatening. I closed my eyes.

As it wriggled its way south the uneven surface of the road bumped us up and down or threw us from side to side. Nowhere did it seem wide enough to accommodate both us and the huge lorries that came hurtling towards us. I cringed, expecting that at any moment we would be thrown in the ditch. But we came to no harm.

Soon we were turning off the main road, which was narrow enough, on to a road that was even narrower. Signposts told the traveller where passing places were. We climbed up and over a hill covered with deep black scars where peat had been dug. A few sheep grazed between the peat banks on what looked to be very poor pickings. Gambolling about among them were one or two lambs, tiny things with sweet faces.

As we crossed the hill the view widened out. There was the sea again, we had only just left it, it had been beside us while we were on the main road just half a mile back. About a mile in front of us was a village, the sea beyond and an island beyond that.

'That village is Bigton,' said Slim. 'It's got a shop, a Post Office, a Church and a village hall. Eddie lives there and so does Alex Smith, another man I work with. The island is St. Ninians. It's joined to the mainland by a strip of sand.'

We made a right turn before we got to Bigton and were on another narrow road through a valley. Away to our left was a small village which Slim told me was called Ireland. At intervals along the road there were small stone built houses, one of which was thatched and looked very quaint.

After a while Slim said, 'Look over there,' and pointed to the other side of the valley. 'That's where you're going to live... eventually.'

I looked, and there was the ruin we had looked at in December. Slim had bought it.

'It will give me something to do in my time off,' he said.

I groaned. From past experience I knew all too well that I was going to be hod carrier, plumber's mate and odd jobber to him as boss, that I too was going to be totally involved in his renovation plans. It was a relief when at last he slowed the van and pulled off the road.

'Everybody out, we're home,' he said.

The cottage Slim had rented was one of a group of four. At the end of the road were some more houses, beyond them a beach and the sea... again.

The first few days in my new home were something of a novelty. Finding homes for the few things we had brought with us didn't take long. The cottage was small and consisted only of two bedrooms, sitting room, minute kitchen, shower and toilet. The kitchen contained nothing more than a cooker and sink unit, there was no room for anything else. The room was so small I could stand in it and touch all four walls without moving my feet, but the view from its window was magnificent. Looking north a sheet of clear water shimmered and sparkled and stretched far into the distance. To the right, steep rocky cliffs reached up to bare hills. Low, undulating land bordered the water to the left. At night time the lights, of what I was later to discover was the town of Scalloway, twinkled brightly and reflected in dancing fingers on the water.

April gave way to May and one day drifted into another. Michael had been enrolled in the school at Dunrossness and every morning at eight thirty was picked up and bussed away, not to return until four in the afternoon. Slim was working shifts, alternating between early and late and seemed to be either working or sleeping.

My life became solitary and the days began to drag. I realised I was homesick when the high spot of my life was the arrival of the postman bringing a letter from my mother. I missed her but I was missing the springtime too, trees putting on fresh green, warmer days, blue skies, primroses and bluebells. Violets, white and blue, would be blooming in the hedgerows. May is the month when the nightingale sings, that small brown bird, hidden in a thorn bush somewhere, sings with a voice so liquid and beautiful, sweeter by far than any other. And I was missing the clamour of the dawn chorus, from the first tentative piping of the blackbird to the full choir giving a rumbustious greeting to the day.

But spring or not, I was lonely and I needed company. I had met my immediate neighbours but they were all pensioners. There was Lizzie, a tall spare old lady who had married twice and outlived both her husbands. There was Bobbie Smith. He had been a crofter/fisherman and had lived in the Maywick valley all his life. Sheep, he told me, were the most stupid animals. 'They never think of anything but eating,' he said. 'There is all this beautiful scenery around them and do you know, they do nothing but put their heads down and eat.'

And then there was Miss Brodie. Miss Brodie had planned to come to Shetland with her sister but her sister had died suddenly and Miss Brodie had bravely decided to make the move on her own. Not long after she arrived she had fallen and broken her hip, so now, not only was she alone but crippled too.

They were nice these neighbours but all were elderly, I needed to get out, meet some younger people and widen my circle of friends. There is no time like the present so I called the dog, shut the door and set off.

There was only one way to go for there was only one road in and out of the valley. I walked south along the eastern side of it. To my left the fields were steep and reached up to meet the rough ground of the hill. Rushes abounded indicating poor, wet land. Tumbling innocently over the rocks in the bed of a deep gully, a little stream of clear water chuckled happily on it's journey to the sea. To my right the land sloped gently down to the valley floor where a loch of dark water brooded silently. Untroubled by wind it mirrored the sky. A narrow strip of water, I judged it to be about a half mile long. From it a stream flowed north.

On the far side of the valley the land climbed again, the lower slopes green but giving way to rough ground higher up. Tucked into the side of the hill there, were three croft houses, all in varying states of decay. One was the house that Slim and I had looked at and which he had subsequently bought. It was long and low, looked dark and deserted. As I stood and gazed at it I wondered if and when I would ever live there.

The day was quiet and serene, a solitary bird floated in the sky above, a vast expanse stretching up from wide horizons. From somewhere far away came the phut-phutting of an engine, the faint sound of voices carried on the air, someone was busy, but the countryside around me was deserted and I felt very alone.

But I was out in search of people so I called the dog, who was snuffling in the ditch investigating all sorts of exciting smells, to follow me and set off again. Sheep and lambs in the fields by the roadside turned tail and fled at our approach and as I had met no-one so far I guessed that not many walkers came that way. The road was long and houses few. Built of local stone they had been constructed in the same style as the ruin Slim had bought. I guessed they also had no more than two or three rooms. They were single storey dwellings with slate or felt roofs. Some were empty and some showed signs of occupation but even these appeared to be locked up and devoid of life. At almost every one there was a dog penned in an outhouse which, at the sound of my footsteps, began to bark frantically, never stopping until I was well away from it.

So far the houses had been well spaced apart but now I came to a group of three. The first had a small barn beside it. A tractor stood outside. A small patch of lawn edged with some flower beds sloped down to the house, which looked well cared for. A little further on another house stood on rising ground above the road. No flowers or lawn here and from the bleak look of its windows I thought it might be unoccupied.

The third house stood by the side of the road. This was the one with the thatched roof I had seen before. It was a small house. Two windows were set in walls no higher than the door. Another tiny window in the roof peeped out from under a bushy brow. The thatch didn't look as though it had been put on in the way I had seen in the south of England but seemed to have been thrown on anyhow. Strings or ropes had been cast over the roof, weighted down with rocks at the ends, presumably to keep the thatch in place. Not even the hayricks would have been thatched like this at home. I decided to find out how the thatcher went about his work. In front of the house the forecourt was of cobble stones, the ground beyond rising steeply to some outhouses on the bank above. Facing the house on the other side of the forecourt were the tumbled down walls of some other buildings. The same thorny roses that I had seen by other houses had sprung up between the stones, softening the outlines.

There was still no sign of people and I wondered where they all were.

I walked on and a little way past the houses I saw a goat. It lay sunning itself on a grassy bank. It got up when it saw me and bleated a greeting. I stopped to speak to her – I could see she was a female – and although our conversation was rather one-sided we got on quite well. She did not appear to be of pedigree stock. Her coat was rough and a rather grubby shade of white. The hair on her knees and hocks had been rubbed away to leave patches of bare skin which looked like brown leather. A pair of horns curved up and back over her head and the tuft of hair beneath her chin waved rhythmically from side to side as she chewed her cud. She seemed to be friendly but as I was not familiar with the habits of goats I kept my distance. I did not fancy being butted by those horns, innocent though her eye may have been.

The noise of a motorcycle being started intruded on my tête-à-tête with the goat. The sound grew louder, it was coming my way, and then it came in sight. It travelled at a speed not much faster than a man could walk, then chugged to a stop beside me. The rider dismounted, smiled and said, 'Good Morning.' He propped the bike up by the side of the road, then took off the helmet he was wearing. His hair was well laced with grey. Rosy cheeks glowed in a skin weathered and lined from exposure to the elements. Black rimmed spectacles circled his eyes.

'Were you looking at the goat?' he asked.

Well, wasn't that obvious? 'Yes. I was,' I said. 'Is it yours?'

6

He was standing beside me now and I could see he was not much taller than I. He took a hand rolled cigarette out of an old tobacco tin, lit it with a match and drew deeply on it before saying, 'It is.'

'Do you keep it for milk?'

'Well, I used to.' He puffed again at his roll-up, then shook his head. 'Ah, but it's a poor old thing now.'

'I've been told that goat's milk is good for people with asthma,' I said. 'My boy has asthma. Where could I get a goat? Do you know?'

'Oh. You could get one.' It was not said with much conviction. 'Put an ad in the paper. Yeh.' He sounded surprised to think he had found the answer to my question.

But I wanted to know more. 'How much would I have to pay for one?'

'I dunna ken. Not much, I'd say.'

We stood there in the sunshine, he with his arms folded, a cigarette burning between brown, smoked stained fingers and I with my hands stuffed into my coat pockets. When she realised she was no longer the centre of attention the goat got fed up and wandered off to lie down in the sun again. Her owner seemed to be in no hurry and I presumed, rightly, that he was yet another pensioner. He told me his name was Bobbie Mullay, and that he lived with his wife, Mary Belle, in the red roofed bungalow a few hundred yards further along the road. We could see it from where we stood. We talked about Shetland, the weather, who I was, where I'd come from and why. He spoke with a broad Shetland accent and used many dialect words which were totally foreign to me. I had to listen carefully in order to understand.

'Well, I have to go,' I said at last and when Bobbie had made me promise that I would call in and visit Mary Belle when next I was passing, I turned to go. Bobbie rode off in the direction he had come and I knew that he had seen me from his home and had come out to have a look at me. It mattered not for I had enjoyed meeting and talking to him. I had made a friend.

BABY

CHAPTER TWO

We had gone up to Yawfield to start clearing out some of the rubbish and I was delving into the back of the box beds in our ruin when Slim came in to join me.

'I've got some bad news Millie,' he said. 'I've been talking to Jimmy and he says that we won't get any mains water up here.'

Jimmy Milliken and Wendy lived in the little house just down the hill from ours. I turned to look at Slim and was surprised to see how serious he looked.

'How does he know that?' I asked.

'Because his supply is very erratic, sometimes he gets no water at all and we're above the level of the reservoir at Geosetter.'

My heart sank. A house with no water is worse than a pub with no beer.

'No water? What on earth are we going to do then?'

'I don't know.'

'But we can't live in a house with no water.'

Slim scratched his head and thought for a moment or two. 'We could put in a pump to drive it up the hill I suppose,' he said

'And how much would that cost?'

'No idea.'

Suddenly all the enthusiasm I'd had when I started just drained away. I looked at all the bits and pieces lying about and thought about the time we would have to spend clearing up before any work could be started. If we couldn't get any water to the house then it would all be wasted effort.

'I don't know about you Slim,' I said. 'But I don't feel like doing any more, let's go home.'

We walked down the hill, crossed the little plank bridge over the stream, climbed up the other side and went home for tea. Afterwards Michael went off to play with a friend, Slim went to work and I crossed the road to pay Bobbie Smith a visit.

I knocked on his door, opened it and called out, 'Hello Bobbie, can I come in?'

As I knew I would be I was invited to step inside. After the usual exchanges and the inevitable cup of tea Bobbie asked me how we were getting on.

I pulled a long face. 'It's all a disaster Bobbie,' I said. 'We've got no water up at the croft.'

'No water? Of course you have.'

'Well, where is it then? Jimmy says that the mains won't reach us.'

'But you have a well.'

'A well? Where?'

'Up by your top gate.'

I have to admit I laughed then. 'D'you mean that puddle? It's only two foot deep and you know what they say about wells on the top of a hill.'

'They can say what they like but that well never dried up as long as I can remember. Other people's did, but that one, never. It's fed by a spring.'

So we did have water. I suppose if we'd thought long and hard enough about it we would have realised that no-one would have built the houses there if there hadn't been a water supply.

'Are you sure about that Bobbie?' How could I possibly have doubted him?

'I'm sure. All the people in the valley used to go to that well for water when theirs were dry.'

'Bless you,' I said. 'You've taken a great load off my mind.'

He smiled. 'I'm glad about that. Now, are you going to dig your peat for the winter?'

'I don't know. I don't think we know how or where to get it.'

'There'll be a peat bank on the hill behind your house. The man you bought the house from will show you where. Aah, but you will get warm cutting it, warm stacking it and warm carrying it home but you won't get so much warmth from the fire.'

'Why? What's wrong with it, doesn't it give out much heat?' I was learning a lot.

'Peat burns splendidly in a Rayburn but slowly on an open hearth. It's free for the taking though, if you discount the hours of work it takes to cut and dry it. Coal is expensive because it has to be brought in by boat and with the exception of driftwood and old fence posts, logs are not to be had.'

Bobbie told me we would need a tushkar, a certain kind of spade for cutting peat. He still went to the hill to cut his winter fuel but now that he was retired had help to get it home. With all the information he had given me I felt in a much better frame of mind. But it was time for me to be off and I said I'd have to go, but before I could he said, 'Come and look at this.'

'This' was just about the smallest lamb I had ever seen. It was lying in a box and was so still I thought it was dead.

'Where did you get that?' I asked.

'I'd been on the hill and saw the birds making a great fuss so I went to see what they were doing. The lamb's mother was dead and the birds were attacking this little thing. I doubt if it will live.'

So it *was* still with us but he was probably right in that it seemed it wouldn't have long to live. The birds had pecked its eyes and head and if Bobbie had not come along when he did they would have killed and eaten it.

'Take it,' he said, picking up the box and thrusting it into my hands. 'Take it for the boy. I have nursed more lambs in my life than I care to think about. Give it a tablespoon of warm milk every hour through the day and night. No more or you will kill it.'

Thanking him for the gift I wondered if there was any chance that the lamb might survive. The thought of getting up every hour through the night was not a happy one but if that was what had to be done, I would try. 'For the boy,' Bobbie had said but I couldn't see 'the boy' rising from his slumbers to feed a lamb.

I said goodbye to Bobbie and carried the box across the road to my house. I set it on the kitchen floor while I warmed some milk in a pan. Lifting the lamb's tiny head I dribbled some milk into its mouth. On examination I thought that the birds had taken one of its eyes right out for it was crusted over and impossible to tell if there was an eye there at all.

Every hour I warmed some milk and fed the little thing. It didn't seem to be able to swallow so I trickled milk off a teaspoon into the side of its mouth hoping that some of it at least would reach its stomach. After each feed I laid the limp little head down on its bed of straw. Hopefully I watched for any sign that the lamb was recovering its strength, but there was none.

Afternoon turned to evening and then to night. Rising hourly from my bed I continued the feeding routine. Morning found me exhausted but the hourly feeds went on throughout the day. Night came again and with it time for bed. I could hardly keep my eyes open. I was not looking forward to another broken night especially as the lamb still lay in the box like a dead thing and did not appear to be making any progress at all.

'Listen Millie,' said Slim. 'It is only a lamb after all and Bobbie did tell you he didn't think it would live. If it's going to make it, it will. You need some sleep, if you wake up, get up, but not every hour.'

I was desperately tired and though hating the thought that the lamb might die if I didn't get up to feed it I went to bed and was asleep as soon as my head hit the pillow. But suddenly I was wide awake. The light was on and Slim was sitting up, grinning widely.

'Come on Mother, baby's calling,' he said.

Maa. The voice was thin and reedy and was coming from the direction of the kitchen. Maa. There it was again. It was the lamb.

I was out of bed in a flash, pushing my feet into my slippers and running to the kitchen. The lamb was standing up in its box. Maa, it called again. It was hungry. I warmed a double portion of milk and fed it. This time the little animal did not flop lifelessly when I put it down but settled itself comfortably. With a sigh of relief I went back to bed and did not wake again until morning.

From that day on I was sure our new pet was going to be all right. With each step it took its wobbly legs grew stronger and soon it was out of the box and trying to follow me round the house. But inside the house is no place for such an animal so it was tethered on the lawn by day and taken into an outhouse for shelter at night. It needed a name and Slim said that as she continued to call me Ma she should be called Baby, so Baby she became.

Baby continued to thrive and soon became one of the family. She joined me and the dog on our walks. When we went to the beach she came with us. She even followed me into the sea one day when we went for a swim, she didn't stay in long but ran back to where we had left our clothes. It was mine she laid on and made soaking wet.

As a family we are all fond of animals and enjoyed the pets we had. Soon they were to be joined by another.

'Mum. Mum, where are you?' Michael, home from school, burst into the house, eyes shining, face alight with excitement. 'Bobbie up the road has given me his goat.'

'Oh no.' I groaned. My idea of a goat had been something a little more presentable than that moth eaten old animal. 'Oh Mike,' I said. 'Not that old thing. What are we going to do with it? Where can we put it?'

My negative approach dampened his enthusiasm not one bit.

'Put her on a tether like Baby,' he said.

I had grave doubts as to whether the owner of the cottage we were renting would agree to a goat on her grass. But it would have been rude to refuse the gift and Michael was so excited that I agreed to go with him to fetch it home. Armed with a piece of rope to lead her with we went along the road. Bobbie flatly refused any offer of payment. 'Take it, for the boy,' he said. Was anything else going to be given us 'for the boy' I wondered. I thanked Bobbie and when he smiled the thought did cross my mind that maybe, just maybe, he was glad to be rid of it.

With the rope fixed to the goat's collar Michael very proudly led his new possession on to the road. The animal was quite amenable and appeared to have no objection to being led away from the bank where she spent most of her time. Nanny, for that was her name, did not make a very pretty picture and I was still a little dubious as to how she might behave so I very wisely walked behind. We got home with no untoward incidents. Slim found a wooden peg to hammer into the ground, tied the rope to it and Nanny was tethered.

Our pets had now grown to three in number. First was our dog, named Shag because of his shaggy coat, second was Baby the lamb and third was Nanny the goat. I should have guessed it would not stop there and sure enough, only a day or two after Nanny joined us, Slim came home with a big grin on his face.

'Here's something to tangle with your knitting,' he said. He put his hand into the front of his anorak and pulled out a tiny black and white kitten. I love cats and put out my hand to take it.

'Hello little one,' I said only to be met with a snarl and a swear. Wow. This one's a character, it must be a tom. It was and we christened him with the entirely unoriginal name of Thomas. He was not very big but what he lacked in size he made up for in confidence. He was afraid of nothing and had not been with us more than a couple of days when I caught him stalking Nanny.

It was summer time now, though the days were not long and hot and sunshine and blue skies could not be guaranteed. Coming from Cornwall where, in summer, driving on crowded roads was a nightmare; shopping, a battle with slow moving sightseers and beaches crowded with hot and fractious holiday makers, the empty roads in Shetland were a pleasure; shopping enjoyable and deserted beaches a dream. I felt as though I had stepped back in time and that life here was being lived in the way I remembered it back in my childhood.

I was especially happy for Michael in that he too could enjoy a childhood free of restrictions. He had become great friends with Bobbie Smith and when we missed him it was to Bobbie's house we first went to look for him. Bobbie had taught him how to play cards and the two were often involved in a game of some kind. Besides learning how to be a card sharp Michael often went down to Maywick beach.

One day when I was cleaning the kitchen I heard the sound of running feet. Someone was in a hurry and it was a breathless Michael who came tumbling through the door.

'Whatever's wrong?' I gasped.

'Mum, Mum, come quick. There's a seal down in the bay.' He was tugging at my sleeve. 'Come on.'

I had only seen seals in a zoo and needed no second bidding to abandon what I was doing. With no crumb of guilt at dereliction of duty I followed him out of the door and together we ran the few hundred yards to the beach. The sea was blue-green and beautiful. Waves rolled in and fell on the sand with a muffled roar. But of the seal there was no sign.

'Where did you see it Mike?' I asked.

'I was walking along and saw a head in the water,' he said. 'I thought it was a swimmer so I said hello but I got no answer. I walked on and I still thought it was a swimmer 'cos it kept up with me. I said hello again but I still got no answer. Then I stopped and looked at it and then I realised it was a seal and then's when I came to get you.'

I scanned the sea's surface hoping to see a head pop up somewhere but the seal must have had other business to attend to for there was no sign of it.

'Never mind,' I said. 'I expect it will come back again some time.'

'Spec it will,' he replied.

'I have heard they like it if you sing to them,' I said.

He laughed. 'Well you'd better not then or we'll never see any.'

'You cheeky monkey.'

I chased after him but he was faster than I and was away up the beach. He had taken his shoes off so I took mine off too and, with our toes we made patterns in the wet sand. We searched the rocks at the foot of the cliffs in case we might find anything exciting but only found driftwood, empty plastic bottles and bits of string. We looked for winkles in the rock pools, watched gulls as they floated on the up-draughts rising up the face of the cliffs. We did what everyone seems to do and no-one seems to know why, we threw pebbles into the sea. I had forgotten about what I was supposed to be doing at home, it didn't seem to matter though and anyway it was much nicer to be in the company of my son, just messing about.

Thomas grew fast and soon changed from a little ball of fluff into a sleek black cat with a white bib. If he had been confident as a kitten he was even more so as a cat. Not only did he tangle with my knitting as Slim had said he would but he was into anything and everything. He fought back with gusto if teased.

Tom's favourite sport was to harass Nanny. He would sit on the garden path and watch her as she grazed. When she had got used to him being there, didn't see him as a threat and turned her back on him, he would race up behind her and leap into the air, all four feet spread-eagled. You could almost hear him yell ya-boo. Nanny would jump in the air with fright then make a dash for safety but she always forgot about her tether and without fail was thrown into reverse like a yo-yo on the end of it. Catching her breath she would glare at Thomas then make a mighty rush at him, head down, horns menacing, obviously intending to impale him on the end of them. But Thomas was too clever for her. He would be just out of reach and would sit there, a smug look on his face and watch as once again Nanny would do a rapid and no doubt painful u-turn. She never learned.

It wasn't only Thomas who took a delight in teasing Nanny. I was across the road at Miss Brodie's house one day when, glancing out of the window my eye was caught by a movement in my garden. Nanny was tethered there. Going to the window to get a better look I saw her standing still but looking toward the outhouse. Then she moved back a few steps, put her head down and charged. From where I stood I couldn't see what was bothering her, probably only Tom, but it was obvious there was something for she charged again.

'Something seems to be bothering the goat,' I said to Miss Brodie. 'Can I go into your bedroom so that I can see what it is?'

'Of course you can,' she said.

The bedroom window gave me a wider view of my garden and to my surprise I saw Slim. He was holding a hessian sack and had it spread out by his side like a toreador's cape. He gave it a shake. Nanny took a couple of steps back, put her head down and charged.

'Ooooh. Slim, you beast.' I ran back to Miss Brodie's sitting room. 'Would you believe it,' I cried. 'Slim's pretending to be a bullfighter and he's using Nanny as a bull. Excuse me while I go and wring his neck.'

'Let me know how you get on,' chuckled Miss Brodie.

I rushed out of the house, ran across the road and was just in time to hear Slim shout, 'Ole' and to see Nanny charge yet again. I thumped Slim and told him to stop it, picked a bunch of the honeysuckle that grew on the garden wall and fed it to the goat as a sort of consolation.

We never did get any milk from her but where she failed in that department she more than made up for in entertainment value. We often tethered her by the side of the road and as traffic using it amounted to no more than two or three vehicles a day we knew she would come to no harm.

Nanny had lost her grubby winter coat and was dressed in new white which made her look quite attractive. Some visitors to Bobbie's house must have thought so too for after picking a large bunch of honeysuckle they, hands outstretched, went to greet her. Nanny bleated her pleasure and promptly ate their bouquet.

One day as she lay in the middle of the road in the sunshine, waggling her ears, chewing her cud and waving her beard in the process, a car approached with people who wanted to go to the beach. The driver tooted his horn. Nanny turned to see what was making the noise but stayed where she was. One by one the passengers got out of the car to try to persuade her to move. They were not bearing gifts however and Nanny was disinclined to co-operate. She did stand up to face them but the travellers were not goat orientated it seemed and fear of this strange animal made them admit defeat. The car was turned around and driven back the way it had come. Bobbie had watched all this from his window while we had sat indoors unaware of the little drama being played out on the highway.

The first few weeks and months of our new life in Shetland was a period of adjustment for us all. After the hustle and bustle of life in the south of England the slower pace of life we were experiencing now was balm to our souls.

But every cherry has its stone.

My first shock came when I went shopping for groceries. I was amazed at the prices being charged. At home I had been paying sixteen pence for a pound of apples and now I was being asked sixteen pence for just one. Pears were the same. Ruefully I thought of the free windfall apples and pears I used to get. Milk was another surprise. Sealed in plastic bags it came up from Scotland and at every stop the delivery van made on its way out from Lerwick the price increased by one penny. I thought the charges were extortionate, thought I was being ripped off and decided not to pay them. For several weeks my shopping basket was woefully empty. I complained loudly to all the shopkeepers only to get the same answer from each one.

'It has to come up on the boat you see.'

It was the cost of freight carried by P & O that increased the price of commodities so much. From then on I virtually closed my eyes to the price tags on most goods, if I wanted something I either had to pay for it or go without.

If shopping was expensive and a shock to the system there were other more pleasant things to compensate. Crime was negligible, cars and houses could safely be left unlocked. Children were free to roam though dire warnings were given that they might be captured by Trows if they went near the peat banks, or the cliffs which were inclined to crumble and were dangerous. Work went on apace through the long summer days but winter saw an easing of pressure and time to spare for socialising so the village hall was well used.

Winter, long and dark as well as damp and cold, brought problems. The cottage we were living in was damp and hard to heat and Michael, who already suffered from asthma was continually getting colds. I too had been no stranger to bronchitis in the past. Despite the shortage of accommodation I pleaded with Slim to try to find us somewhere else to live.

'I'll see what I can do,' he said.

M. VIGOR

CHAPTER THREE

The prospects of finding somewhere else to live were not good, the oil boom had brought oil-related workers pouring in to the islands and houses to rent were in very short supply. But we were in luck, an estate of new houses had been built near the airport. We applied for and were allocated one.

The houses were modern, architect designed and had cost a great deal of money to build. Three bedrooms opened off a large hall. Lounge, dining and kitchen areas were open plan. The fireplace in the lounge was unfinished, a grate had been fitted but the surround had to be supplied by the tenants.

Arrangements were made to get our furniture out of store and brought to the new address and by autumn we were settled in at Thistle Court. Michael would still go to the same school, Slim would have a shorter journey to work and I would exchange the view from my kitchen window from Clift Sound to Quendale Bay. What could be better?

We had brought bags of peat with us from Yawfield and as the weather had turned colder decided to light a fire.

'I'll do it,' said Slim.

Instantly I remembered being told how, when he was on leave at his parents', his mother had come home from work to find a fire engine parked outside and the men sitting in the kitchen drinking tea. Slim had set fire to the chimney. That was a long time ago but still I crossed my fingers, then uncrossed them, after all what harm could he do just lighting a fire in a grate.

He likes lighting fires. I watched as he built it carefully, struck a match, then sat back to watch. All went well and the fire burned brightly, there must be a good draught, we thought. But then it went dull. There was a smell of smoke in the house though none was visible in the room. Something must be on fire, we thought, so we searched everywhere only to find nothing. I suggested it must be to do with the direction of the wind or something and went to put Michael to bed.

When I opened the airing cupboard door to get his clean pyjamas I was enveloped in a cloud of acrid smoke. I shouted to Slim that I had found the seat of the fire, but no, there was still no fire, just a cupboard full of smoke.

'D'you think something is blocking the chimney Slim?' I asked.

'Looks like it. I'll go out and have a look.'

He was gone only seconds and came back laughing.

'You've got to come and see this,' he chortled. 'I think we must be doing forty knots.'

I had to laugh too when I saw columns of smoke coming out of the air bricks round the foot of the house. Nothing was coming out of the chimney at all. We blamed air pressure then, and down draught, but still thought it strange that smoke went under the floorboards and out through the walls and didn't come into the room.

The wind and rain that make up a great deal of Shetland's weather did nothing for any attempt on my part to look well turned out. The use of an umbrella for protection became a liability, the wind tended to turn it inside out with alacrity. Woolly hats were a necessity, nothing else being secure enough to stand the buffeting of the wind. Essential too were warm overcoats but, like woolly hats, soaked up the rain like a sponge. Plastic macs were an abomination, rain gathered in little rivers on them, ran down to funnel into and fill rubber boots. There had to be something better.

There was! It was called an anorak. Made of navy blue nylon, with a padded lining for warmth and a hood with a fur edging, it was just the thing. It was light but warm, easily dried when wet and available in a wide range of sizes to fit everyone from a toddler to an all-in wrestler.

Anoraks and denims became standard dress. I didn't like it for it did nothing for individuality and as for smartness, well, they were non-starters. I swore I would not be seen dead in one and resisted strongly all attempts to be convinced that they were the in thing. Slim and Michael had been quickly taken over by the anorak and despite my initial resistance I too had to agree that for warmth and comfort, there was nothing better than to be wrapped in it's cosy cocoon.

The anorak turned out to be an excellent piece of apparel despite one flaw. When the hood was up and the drawstring tied under the chin the wearer was effectively blinkered. Line of vision was forward only, to look right or left the whole body had to be turned. Many a person who forgot this and turned the head rapidly right or left, soon learned what the inside of the anorak hood looked like. It was not an endearing sight.

There was one other drawback to it. Favoured garment of men, women and children, it made identification difficult for unless one was face to face with a person it was not easy to tell one gender from the other.

November brought a few flurries of snow, but the salty air coming off the sea soon made it disappear. I was told that snow never stayed long in Shetland but the end of the month brought a cold wind from the east and a heavier fall. Thick white flakes fell steadily until all was covered. During the night there was a heavy frost. Next day more snow fell. Roads became coated with a thick, hard packed layer. In spite of this there were still some intrepid travellers out and about, their cars probably equipped with steel studded tyres which would give a better grip. I decided that discretion was the better part of valour, stoked the fire and stayed at home.

Our house was on a hillside and only a wire fence divided the garden from the hill. Soon the white clad slope was peppered with small figures pulling or riding toboggans. I stood at my sitting room window and watched as daredevil children came hurtling down the hill towards me. Many times I thought they would come straight through the fence and the window to join me indoors. But just beyond the fence was a deep depression, filled now with snow and levelled off. The unsuspecting tobogganer who failed to leap off in time was thrown willy-nilly into it.

Because of the bad weather we had not been to Yawfield for two days. I knew that the hay rack had been well filled the last time we were there but I was concerned lest the water supply had frozen. Besides being concerned about the animals I was worried about my mother. News had come that she was not well.

I had booked a flight for the following Tuesday and there were only a couple of days left before I was due to go. I wondered how long the snow would last and if it would stop us going up to see to the animals before I went away.

'Do you think we ought to go up to the croft ?' I asked Slim when he came home off night shift.

'It's not very good for driving.'

'But everyone else is, it can't be that bad.'

Cars were still moving on the roads and men were getting to work. We discussed what we should do and after some deliberation decided to make an attempt. As it was now mid-morning I put a leg of lamb in the oven to start cooking while we were away. Leaving Michael with a friend we started out.

Driving down the road towards the village was OK but when we reached the main road, a turning at the side of steep Wart Hill, we stopped and stared. The road was covered with a thick layer of snow and ice. Neither Slim nor I liked the look of it and decided that when a JCB that was coming up the hill had passed by we would turn round and go home.

The JCB came abreast of us and stopped, the driver opened his door and called out.

'D'you want to go up the hill?'

'Well, not really.'

But he said. 'I'll give you a tow if you like.' And like fools we said, 'OK.'

Once on the top of the hill we found that grit and salt had been spread and the going was easy. We got to the croft without incident and once there, re-filled the hay racks, saw that there was water, and happy that Nanny and Baby were fit and well and that we had done what was required, set off for home again.

From Yawfield, to Sumburgh and Thistle Court, the road wended its way between the few houses at Ireland and through the village of Bigton. Between Bigton and the next township of Scousburgh it was narrow and winding and as we neared Scousburgh the steep flank of a hill rose up on one side while on the other there was a sheer drop to the sea. There were no safety barriers, just a post and wire fence. Though safely strapped in I was full of apprehension, afraid that we might skid on an icy patch and slide into eternity in a very nasty way. I only felt safe when we reached the main road at Robin's Brae. From then on the road ran through reasonably level farmland and was wide enough for two cars to pass each other without either having to give way.

The ever-present wind blew small flurries of snow across the road and from time to time a gust would make the van shiver. It made me nervous and I wished I was already at home. Then disaster struck.

We were at the top of a small incline and passing a house on our right. There was a gap between it and an outbuilding and as we were going by a blast of wind came charging through between them and sent the van waltzing down the road. The surface of the road was icy smooth, there was nothing on which the tyres could make purchase.

The tail of the van slid left, straightened momentarily then swung right. I held my breath. Left again. Then right. Straight. Left, left. Too long. We were broadside on and all control was lost. I clung tightly to the handle above the door, my other hand trying to get a grip on the fascia. I was now looking at a grassy bank with a wall behind it. Slowly, oh so slowly it seemed, the van slid towards it. I could see that the long grass of the verge, which was on the sheltered side of the wall, was standing stiff and motionless and practically devoid of snow.

And then the van hit the bank head on, stood on its nose momentarily then fell heavily on its side and slid backwards down the hill. Through the window of the passenger door I could see, a few inches from my face, the grass being crushed beneath the weight of the van and pulled into parallel lines of green, white and brown as it went. The door of the glove compartment flew open and instinctively I put up my arm to shield my face. Something hit me on the elbow and other small objects rained about me.

Then everything stopped. The vehicle was at a standstill and we were alive.

'Come on Millie, we must get out.'

Slim had opened the driver's door and was climbing out. I looked up to see him sitting outside, his feet dangling just above my head. He leaned forward and held a hand out to me.

'Give me your hands,' he said. 'I'll help you. Come on, in case it goes on fire.'

I scrambled to my feet, lifted my arms, well, my right one anyway, the left one wouldn't move. It gave me no pain but something was obviously wrong.

'I think I've broken my collar bone,' I said and knew that I had.

Somehow Slim got me out of the van and we stood by the road side and looked at our poor Volkswagen lying on its side. The back door had been thrown open by the impact and tools and bits and pieces were strewn across the road. The dog too had been thrown out but he was on his feet and had come to no harm. I stood there and nursed my arm and wondered what we were going to do next. No-one seemed to be aware that we were in difficulties even though there was a house on one side of the road and a farm on the other. But it was Sunday, a cold November day and it was nearly lunchtime.

Samaritans come in all sorts of shapes and sizes. The first to arrive were some workmen in a van. They stopped to see if we needed help and offered to take me to our doctor for emergency treatment. Helping me into the passenger seat of their van they made me as comfortable as possible and assured Slim they would take every care of me.

We were about to set off when a second set of Samaritans arrived, a local builder and his wife. They drove a Range Rover.

'We'll take you,' they said.

I was removed from the van and transferred to what was deemed to be a superior vehicle. Though it probably was safer than the workmen's van it was not as comfortable for the seat was hard and unyielding.

At the surgery the doctor, who must have been about to sit down to his Sunday lunch, was kind and sympathetic.

'Let's see what you've been doing,' he said as he started to help me off with my jacket. Under the jacket I wore a thick Aran jumper, a thin jumper, a cotton blouse and a vest. He smiled as he asked, 'Do you feel the cold?'

'Yes I do. I haven't been warm since I got here.'

It was true. I just could not seem to keep warm. Slim swore that a Shetland winter was not as cold as it could be in the south of England. I was inclined not to believe him.

The doctor confirmed that I had broken my collarbone. He put a bandage in a figure of eight round my shoulders to hold them back, gave me a bottle of pain killers, then sent me home with instructions to go to the hospital at Lerwick the following day.

Once again I climbed into the Range Rover for the journey back. As we passed the spot where the accident had happened I saw that the van had been pulled upright and taken off the road. By the time I got home I was feeling quite chirpy and invited my transport driver and his wife in for coffee, but the husband was looking worried.

'You'd better take it easy,' he said. 'You may get delayed shock.'

'Shock?' I said. 'It was just an accident and nobody was badly hurt.' What's he bothered about, I thought, it was nothing. I made them some coffee, thanked them for coming to my rescue and, in a while, bade them goodbye.

The leg of lamb I had put in the oven before I went out was sending out appetising smells. It was time to check on it. I opened the oven door, picked up a cloth to hold the roasting pan with and came to a full stop. The dish was too heavy, I couldn't lift it with one hand. Neither could I peel the potatoes. In fact I could do very little. With one arm out of commission I was well and truly handicapped.

By the time Slim came home I was feeling very sorry for myself but he assured me that he and Michael could manage fine and that they would look after me. It was my chance to be a lady and do nothing but watch TV all day long.

Well, I could if it was possible to get a picture but TV reception was not very good and certainly not available everywhere in Shetland.

That night I was propped up in bed with lots of pillows and dosed with hot milk and painkillers to help me sleep. I did sleep, but only fitfully and in the morning I woke to a world that had gone a nasty shade of grey. My Samaritan had been right. Without warning shock had hit me right between the eyes. And now I had to face a twenty-mile journey to the hospital for X-rays.

'Look out of the window Millie. The snow is gone.'

Oh fickle weather, what tricks you play. Roads that had been covered with snow and ice the previous day were now black and wet. Had we waited another day to go to the croft we would not have had the accident, I would not have my arm in a sling and I would not have to sit in a chair and feel useless. The animals would not have starved and in one more day I would have been on a plane, winging south. Travel was now denied.

The hospital was like any other hospital, the consultant competent and impersonal. I was X-rayed and re-bandaged and sent home with yet more pills. For several days I was confined to bed and existed in a world that was like a bad dream, something disturbing and uncomfortable that I could not get away from. Once well enough to leave my bed and sit by the fire I was glad when Mimie came to visit. She had called every day – though Slim had not told me – but from then on until I came out of the gloom and began to smile again, she was there.

Gradually I began to do a few jobs round the house. I made beds, though not very tidily, used the vacuum cleaner and the duster, made tea and washed a few dishes.

It was my left shoulder that had received the blow, my right arm was not affected, I was still able to write. I had planned to write about our new life in this northern isle, so now was the time to start. At least I could make notes to refer to later. I wrote to my sister and told her what had happened and by return of post came her reply. She was so sorry to hear about the accident and hoped I would soon be well and to help me pass the time she enclosed a book which she hoped I might enjoy. It was Lillian Beckwith's 'The Hills is Lonely'. I read it and as I turned each page I thought, it's the very same sort of book I had hoped to write. I threw away my pencil and with it any thoughts that I could be a writer, put on my hat and coat and took the dog for a walk.

A telephone call just before Christmas told me that my mother had fallen on the floor during the night and had lain there for several hours. Consequently she was confined to bed and my presence was required. With my arm in a sling I boarded the plane and flew south to see what I could do

Old age can be unkind to the elderly. The little old lady I found at home had become a stranger. She gave me no smile of greeting and there was no look of recognition in her eyes. When I gave her a cup of tea she said, 'Thank you very much,' as though I were a waitress. As I sat by her bed I wondered where my mother had gone.

Childhood memories came flooding back. Mother's firm grip on my hand as she dragged me, wailing loudly in protest, to school. Coming home to find her clad in a white apron, arranging freshly ironed garments on a clothes horse in front of the fire, I remember the smell they gave off to this day. I recalled seeing the worried expression on her face as she struggled to stretch my father's meagre wage to feed her family. When I left school at fourteen years of age she bullied me into taking a job as a kitchen maid saying, "service is good for girls". In an attempt to get my little brother to practice playing the violin she got one for herself but never learnt anything but 'Now the day is over'. Later she developed a passion for the stage and cheerfully abandoned the washing up to learn her lines.

My father had been a meek and gentle man, mother had to be the strong one. What she lacked in feet and inches, stones and pounds, she made up for with guts and determination. When life dealt her body blows she fought back and the words, 'can't' and 'give up' were not in her vocabulary.

The doctor called and, sitting at her bedside with his bag on his lap, told me there was nothing to be done, it was just old age. I stayed on to look after her and when she was well enough to leave her bed, though she lived in a close of bungalows with a warden in attendance, it was with a great deal of reluctance I left to return to Shetland and my family.

In January my mother died. Death of a parent is something that life does not prepare us for. Suddenly there is a void that no-one else can fill. My mother had been there for as long as I could remember, she represented home and safety and now it was gone. I had to learn to accept the things I could not alter and to come to terms with my grief.

Slim cared for and consoled me. After a week or two of my moping round the house with a long face he said, 'I think you ought to get a job Millie.'

CHAPTER FOUR

'What do I want a job for?'

'You spend far too much time on your own. It would be good for you.'

Going back to work was not top of my list of priorities but saying 'No' would encourage Slim to press harder so I said I'd think about it.

'Well, don't think about it too long, they need someone in the kitchen at the Clubhouse.'

'And I suppose you want me to try for it.'

'Why not? You've got plenty of experience. You could do it with one hand tied behind your back.' Oh yes, I've been there, I thought. 'And it would give you some pocket money,' he went on.

'You really want me to get a job don't you? I suppose you had it all worked out right from the start didn't you?'

The answer he gave to that was a great big grin.

I did think about it for a while and, as Slim was on permanent night shift, four on, four off, he slept during the day and for me, having to creep about so as not to disturb him, those days seemed endless. I did need to get out of the house more, the companionship of other people would be good for me and the pocket money would be most welcome. I picked up the phone and made an appointment to be interviewed.

The British Airways Clubhouse was at the top of a hill overlooking the airport and the sweep of water called the West Voe. A social club, it also had bedrooms for aircrews on stopover. I was shown in to the manager's office and was interviewed by Ian, a tall, thin dark haired man. As interviews go it was more like a conversation between friends. I was the only applicant for the job so it was mine without question. Ian showed me where I would work and introduced me to Ronnie Williamson, the chef. As to my catering experience, it was hardly required for I was to wash dishes, prepare vegetables and help cook mountains of chips.

I started work on the following Monday.

Ronnie was a Shetlander. Well built, plump almost, he had a lively sense of humour. We got on well. Many times while he beat some mixture in a basin, while I stood at the sink with my hands immersed in a bowl of suds, he would come to me, nudge me in the ribs and say, 'Have you heard this one?' Then he'd tell me the latest joke and we would both dissolve into fits of laughter.

Ronnie was good for me, being in his company day after day helped to lift my melancholy and bring me back to normality. Though he and I were the only workers in the kitchen, there were housemaids to clean the bedrooms, bar maids in the bar on the floor above the kitchen and Ian, the manager.

At eleven o'clock each morning Ronnie and I downed tools for our morning coffee. The housemaids joined us in our rest area, a table and chairs in a corner of the store room. With our coffee and a plate of drop scones that Ronnie had made for us we all spent a hilarious ten to fifteen minute break. For some reason the bar maids didn't join us but they heard our laughter and asked what it was all about. It was not easy to tell them so we invited them to join us.

It wasn't that we didn't like them or had anything against them but as they walked through the kitchen door next morning sobriety descended on the rest of us. Hilarity evaporated like mist on a midsummer morning. The next ten minutes were long and tedious and we were all relieved when the bar staff left us saying that they still didn't know what we laughed about. There was no explaining the fact that as soon as they were gone the rest of us were laughing again.

As we now lived on an estate our dog, Shag, was not allowed to run free but had to be taken for walks. This was a pleasure rather than a hardship. Quendale Bay, where the sea came rolling in from the south, was just a short walk away. The mile long beach was enclosed on the landward side by an area of sand dunes covered by the tough spears of marram grass. Low rocky cliffs bordered the bay on either side.

Walking on the beach was very therapeutic. Beach combing and wave watching were still my favourite pastimes. Odd things washed up on the shore, bottles, boxes, oil drums, pieces of rope and string, sometimes a shoe or beach sandal. Dead fish, birds and once, a stinking seal round which bluebottles abounded. Scavenging birds patrolled the skies. The sight of them sent Shag berserk. They'd wheel above his head then skim low over the sand inviting him to give chase. Just as it seemed he would close teeth on flesh, with a flap of its wings the bird would soar away into the skies. Its call of keeow, keeow, mocking the breathless dog below.

Birds other than gulls frequented the beach. A swarm of little birds in tight formation, with a rush of wings, dipped, rose and fell again and generally delighted me with their unpredictable flight. On the beach, flocks of other small birds ran twittering before the oncoming sea, then turned to chase it as it fell back again. Time after time they ran before it and chased it back.

On the east side of the bay was a small inlet with a pebbly beach and an outcrop of rocks. It was only accessible at low tide. When the tide was in and seals were in the bay it was a favourite place of theirs. A group of them would lie on the rocks and sunbathe, doze or wave a lazy flipper. I would creep along the cliff top and hope to find them there. If I was lucky I could get a close look at them. They varied in colour, some very dark and some grey and mottled. I had to be very quiet and still so as not to scare them away, but then some false move or sound would alert them to my presence and several pairs of big dark eyes would be turned my way. For a second or two they would stare at me, then one of them would slither down the rock and into the sea and the rest would follow, disappearing with hardly a splash into the water. In a little while a head would surface and once again I would be scrutinised by those liquid eyes. Other heads would appear, then disappear and the seals would turn seaward and be gone. I always felt guilty that I had disturbed their siesta but knew they would return and I'd see them there again.

'Get your overalls on Millie, it's time to get down to some work, we're going up to Yawfield today. We've really got to get going on the house.'

It was Slim's day off and as the weather was fine he didn't want to waste it by staying at home.

'All right,' I said. 'D'you want me to fill a flask and make a sandwich?'

'Could do, but don't be long.'

It was about six miles to Bigton, another mile to Ireland and then a mile and a half of rough pot-holed track to our ruin. We didn't have a car, just a one-ton Volkswagen van, Slim's pride and joy, and, as he said, it would be very useful for fetching and carrying all the sand, cement and timber, etcetera, that we would need. First of all though, we had to make an assessment of what had to be done, and in what order, and that was the purpose of this visit.

From the cottage at Maywick it had been a short walk across the valley to the house and sometimes on Slim's day off we would walk across and look it over. The more we had looked at it the more we realised just how big a task it was going to be to restore it.

Now, as we came over the hill and started the descent to the house I could see it crouched there, black tarred roof scowling above blank eyed windows. Rounding the corner of the outbuildings we came to a stop in front of it, on a grassy, level piece of ground. My feelings at that moment were very mixed. Did I really want to be involved in all this? Did I want to help mix cement, to fetch and carry? And even as I thought it I knew I had no choice.

'Come on, out you get. Let's get on with it. Got your note book?'

Yes, I'd got my notebook and my pencil so out I got and followed Slim.

There were two cottages as well as outbuildings but it was the main cottage we were interested in. It was built in the traditional style, two rooms, but and ben, with box beds making the dividing wall in the middle.

The entrance to the cottage was by way of a porch and from there a door led into the living room or but end. The fireplace in the but end was an open hearth with pot hooks hanging from the chimney. The fire would have been built on the hearth, there being no fire basket. From this room a door led into the ben end. The ben end, we thought, was the parlour, for the fireplace was a modern tiled one. The box beds opened into this room, built of tongue and groove boards they were now in a bad state. The bases of the beds were gone. There had been two, one above the other. Curtains which had been used to disguise what was behind them, hung in shreds. The beds having been put in the middle of the house seemed to be a very good idea for it was surely the warmest and driest place.

The floors of the house were rotten, it was obvious the roof leaked.

'What do you think then Slim?' I asked.

'I think we shall have to gut the whole of the centre of the house and start again. The walls are sound for the most part but I can see daylight between the stones behind the fireplace.'

'Can you?'

'Yes. Now let's go and have a look outside.'

A look at the wall against which the fireplace stood revealed that the mortar between many of the stones was missing, allowing wind and rain to blow straight through. To repair it was a priority job. We stepped back to look up and study the roof. It had, in the past, been covered with some sort of cloth and then tarred. Through time, the cloth had dried and cracked and in some parts was peeling off. It was decided that this was a patch up job as at some later date we thought to put slates on but before we did that one of the chimneys would have to be removed.

'First thing we want is a decent wheelbarrow,' said Slim.

'And some shovels and tough gloves,' said I. 'Get them next time we go into town. In the meantime I'm going to have a poke about indoors.'

In the space where the beds had been were some bags and boxes. Looking into them before throwing them out I was surprised to find clothes and shoes. The shoes dated from the Second World War and still had the old CC41 mark on them. In one of the bags I found the remains of a baby's layette. First things out of the bag were some old fashioned wrappers and long gowns, rather the worse for damp, the attentions of moths and for having lain there so long. The shawl, once silk and wool, had been eaten into holes by moths.

A tin box yielded other treasures. Bills for food. Christmas cards and note books with records of work done on the croft. I called to Slim to come and have a look.

'See this,' I said. 'Ten sheep sold and the total receipt is a penny under £46. And again, eight lambs, £23. That's less than £3 a head. There's lists of breeding stocks of sheep, and look...' I held up an invoice headed J D Williams, Dale Street, Manchester. 'Here's the bill for the baby's layette and mother's maternity dress. One pound ten shillings. That includes a dozen terry nappies and it was only three shillings and six pence for the mother's dress.'

Slim wasn't particularly impressed but I was uncovering the past and I wasn't about to throw it away. I put the papers back in the tin and carried it out to the van, I would have a closer look at it all later.

The small adjoining cottage was in a worse state of repair than the main one. The floor, what was left of it, seemed to be littered with nothing but junk. From among it I rescued some pieces of wood which, when fitted together, made up the frames that were used to dry and shape the hand knitted Fair Isle jumpers. I also picked up four long pieces of wood that were studded with nails. I had no idea what they were for except that I guessed they too were something to do with knitting.

A real treasure unearthed from the pile of rubbish was an old knitting belt. Made of leather and stuffed with horsehair, the pad, which was boat shaped, was perforated with holes on one side. The leather was dry and stiff, I knew I would have to give it a liberal dressing of saddle soap to soften it up. I was delighted with this find because I wanted to learn to knit the colourful Fair Isle patterns. I also wanted to knit in the way they did in Shetland and the knitting belt was an essential item if I was going to do so.

'Look what I've found Mimie,' I said when I next saw her. I showed her my knitting belt. 'Will you teach me how to knit Fair Isle?'

'I will,' she said.

'Where can I buy a pattern then?'

'What do you want to do that for? We have a pattern book you can copy from.'

The book was produced. It was an exercise book of graph paper. The patterns were marked out in squares indicating differing numbers of stitches and looked as one would expect a cross stitch embroidery pattern to be. I couldn't see how it was going to show me how to knit a jumper.

'Looks like a Chinese puzzle,' I said. 'How do I knit a jumper from that? How do I know how many stitches to cast on?'

'It takes fourteen score of stiches for a thirty-six inch chest if you knit to a tension of seven stitches to the inch. The basque, or rib as you would call it, has to be two thirds of the whole.'

Inside the front cover of the exercise book had been written the number of stitches for differing sizes, all in scores of numbers. Mimie explained to me how to 'lay off' stitches for the armhole, that is to put them on a thread and not to cast them off. She also told me how to calculate the number of stitches for the neck and how to graft the stitches together at the top of the shoulder, then to pick up stitches round the armhole and knit the sleeve from top to bottom.

'That way you can knit a new cuff when this one gets worn out.'

I decided that the first jumper I was going to knit would be for Michael, he being the smallest. Wool and needles, of which I needed three, were now at the top of my list for when I next went shopping. I had watched Mimie, needles flying, coloured wools interweaving as she worked at a jumper for one of her family. Her needles were of steel – she called them wires – and the stitches were evenly divided between two and the third one, with its end tucked firmly into the knitting belt for stability, was the working one.

I was keen to get started but knitted the rib on two needles first then transferred them to the 'wires'. Though quite an experienced knitter I found this new style of working very difficult at first. But practice makes perfect, well, hopefully, and when Slim was sleeping after night shift I seized the opportunity to spend several hours at the work. The jumper grew rapidly and within ten days was finished. Mimie was surprised that I had managed to complete it so quickly. She examined it closely and then proclaimed that for a first attempt it was very good. This was praise indeed and from then on the knitting needles were never still.

I had been working at the Clubhouse for quite a while when a vacancy arose at the canteen in the British Airways hanger for a cook supervisor. Thinking I'd like a change of scene I applied for and got it. Kitchen staff consisted of myself and two other women. Alison was a Shetlander, steady and reliable as a rock. Maria was a happy, plump and smiling Argentinian who was married to a Shetland man. She and Alison lived next door to each other and were the best of friends.

The canteen was open from eight in the morning until six at night and was closed after lunch from two o'clock until three so that we could clean up.
The menu I inherited was plain and dreary and the number of meals required was easy to cope with so we were definitely not rushed off our feet.

My previous experience in catering had begun, with what I thought was slavery, as a kitchen maid in a big country house, but it was where I learned the rudiments of cooking for numbers. Much later I became one of the cooks in a busy transport café and later still, when Slim was in the Navy and on the other side of the world on board ship, I opened my house to summer visitors and became a B&B landlady in Cornwall.

Whoever I cooked for, whether rich or poor, it was against my principles to dish up a meal I would not be happy to eat myself so the menu and style of cooking in the BA canteen changed. Among other things we dished up tasty stews, casseroled pork, fresh fish for main meals and for afters, apple pie, rice pudding and, a great favourite, bread and butter pudding. Gradually the numbers coming in for meals increased.

'They're not all British Airways men,' said Maria. 'Do you think we ought to serve them?'

'Unless you want to stand at the door and sort them out I don't think there's anything we can do about it,' I said. 'I don't know who they are, do you?'

Maria shrugged her shoulders and made a face, I did the same and we continued to dish up meals. And still the queue grew longer until it snaked out through the door of the canteen and into the hanger.

The B.A.H. hanger housed not only the helicopters but the offices of the manager, secretarial staff and the chief engineer. There were also crew rooms for the engineers and pilots as well as the canteen. The pilots spent a lot of time sitting in their crew room waiting for a call to make a flight somewhere.

In case they were called out and had to miss a meal they had an allowance of sixty pence per day for emergency food supplies. They still got their allowance even if they weren't called out so they used it to buy sweeties to take home for the kids. For some reason they came to spend their money during the hour the canteen was closed.

At first I let them in when they knocked on the kitchen door but then I decided they should be treated the same as the engineers and only use the canteen during opening hours. The next time a pilot came knocking and asked to get his allowance I refused and told him to come back when we were open. His jaw dropped. His eyes opened wide and his face registered shock and disbelief. He stamped his foot and asked me who I thought I was. I told him and he slammed the door - it opened outwards - in my face. I turned away to get on with my work. Maria and Alison looked at me in amazement.

'You can't do that,' said Maria. 'They're pilots.'

'Pilots? They're just taxi drivers and I just have,' I said. 'And don't you let them in if I'm not here. They only get their sweeties to take home to the kids. We're not closed for pleasure but because we have work to do and what have they been doing? Sitting in the crew room doing nothing. OK?'

It took a little while before all the pilots learned they would not be served during the hour the canteen was closed. Many more times there were tantrums, stamping of feet and slamming of the door. They threatened to report me to management but their rage was futile. I would not budge. At each encounter Alison and Maria put on their serious faces but as soon as the door was closed and locked all three of us would crease up with laughter. We were in a superior position, truly egalitarian, what was sauce for the goose was sauce for the gander.

Though not as cold as one might expect, the weather in Shetland still leaves much to be desired. It rains frequently and the wind blows most of the time. The air seems to be permanently damp. These conditions destroyed any attempts by me to put a curl in my hair. It got wispy and unmanageable and wearing a woolly hat put paid to any style I tried to coax it into. In the end I got fed up with it and decided to have it cut short. Maybe my appearance would then become less bedraggled and windblown.

'You won't have to go far,' said Mimie when I asked her to recommend a hairdresser. 'There's one in the village. I go to her. She's good, but you'll find it different to what you're used to.' She then instructed me how to find her. 'A couple of hundred yards after the road junction, turn right. Go in behind the barn and turn right again. There's a caravan there and that's where the hairdresser lives.'

I followed her instructions to the letter, parked in a space beside the barn and followed a path round it. Behind the barn a collection of bits and pieces of farm machinery, grown in by weeds, were quietly rusting away. The footpath led to a large caravan, its doorway protected by a wooden porch. In its shelter huddled five or six hens and several cats. It seemed an odd sort of place to find a hairdresser's salon.

I knocked on the door and a voice from inside told me to come in. I hesitated, not being used to walking in to a stranger's dwelling. While I stood there dithering the door was opened by a buxom blonde lass.

'Come in, come in. Don't stand on the step. Nobody knocks here.'

She turned and went back inside so there was nothing I could do but follow her.

In the centre of the main room a lady sat on a kitchen chair, her hair partly wound in curlers. A second was under a hair dryer in the corner. On a settee a woman cradled a cat on her lap, another cat slept by her side. Seated on the floor in front of a television set were several small children. The hairdresser turned to me as she continued to put curlers in her customer's hair.

'What was it you wanted?' she asked.

'I want to make an appointment to get my hair cut and permed. Mimie Sinclair recommended you.'

'If you wait 'til I've got this done I'll get my book. Sit you down.'

She indicated the settee and I sat myself next to the lady and the cats.

'It's a bonnie day,' said the lady.

'Yes, it is.'

'You'll be at Thistle Court.'

It was simultaneously a statement and a question. The usual ones as to where had I come from, did I like Shetland, etcetera followed. The children took no notice of me at all but the sleeping cat woke, climbed on to my lap and proceeded to shed hairs on my clothes. When all the curlers were speared in place, a hair net tied on to trap them all and the client ensconced under a second drier, the hairdresser turned to me.

'My name's Lillian,' she said. 'What's yours?'

'Millie.'

'OK, Millie.' She pronounced it Mullie. 'Let's see when we can fit you in.'

An appointment was made and, 'See you soon,' said Lillian. 'You can let yourself out.' She smiled her goodbye and turned back to continue her work.

I opened the door to leave and there in the porch the hens and cats still sat and lay about. With suspicious yellow eyes the cats watched me but the hens just ruffled their feathers and made themselves more comfortable. None moved or ran away as I walked by them.

I had letters to post but no stamps so I drove on down through the village to the Post Office. Housed in a gaunt building it presented a rather grim exterior but once through the front door, the postmistress and her husband dispensed a friendly and efficient service. The incoming mail from the mainland, carried by plane and picked up by the local postman, was brought there first. I bought my stamps, posted my letters and then went to the village shop for some milk.

Goudie's shop was an Aladdin's cave. Groceries, bread, socks and shirts. Bootlaces, knitting wool, jewellery and cosmetics. Papers, magazines and balls of string, it was all there, and more.

My favourite shelves were the ones holding the skeins of wool. All the colours of Shetland spun into something more tangible. The pinks and purples of heather, greens and browns of the hills. All the shades of the sea. The blues and greys of the water, the white of spindrift coming off the waves. The bonnie blue of a summer sky, the yellows of primroses, daffodils and the stiff, straight flag iris by the water's edge. The brown, almost black of the peat.

I wanted to buy it all and knit, knit, knit until I was surrounded by a kaleidoscope of colour. It was easy to see how and why the colourful Fair Isle patterns had come into being. The fleeting hues of summer had been captured to colour the bleakness of long, dark winter days.

On the day of my hair appointment, Slim was first out of bed while I lay there, warm and cosy and reluctant to move. Then he was calling.

'Millie. Get up and come and look at this.'

'What is it?' I asked as I snuggled deeper under the blankets.

'There's a platform adrift in the bay.'

'A *what*?'

My dull morning mind associated platforms with railway stations but trains and stations were non-existent in Shetland. Rolling out of bed I pulled on a dressing gown and shuffled out to the kitchen. Slim was sitting on a stool, gazing seaward through a pair of binoculars. He handed me the glasses.

'Look out there, ' he said.

I looked, and what I saw captured my attention completely.

M. VIGOR

CHAPTER FIVE

The sea was pitching angry waves and being tossed about, as though it were nothing more than driftwood, was an oil exploration platform. A couple of tugs were fussing round it.

'Seems like they've lost the tow line,' said Slim.

On an incoming tide the platform was being driven slowly towards the land. It was in line with a rocky headland and too far east to ground itself on Quendale beach. The situation looked serious.

With the aid of the glasses it was possible to see the tiny forms of men on the rig. The search and rescue helicopter from the airport appeared on the scene, circled, then stopped to hover over it. Unable to tear my eyes away I watched as the winch rope was let down and, one by one, the men were lifted off and carried away.

Somehow a tow line would have to be fastened to the rig if it was to be saved, but now there were no men on it how was that going to be achieved? I didn't want to miss even the smallest piece of the action but Michael had to go to school. Between getting his breakfast and seeing to him my gaze was continually drawn to the window and the drama beyond. Slim, not having to go to work, was in no hurry to abandon his ring side seat.

'Oh, oh. We've got a fire now,' he said. 'Come and look.'

A plume of smoke was rising from one of the tugs and rapidly grew into a thick, black cloud. As I watched, the tug began to go round in circles, the steering mechanism must have been locked. It wasn't long before the rescue helicopter was back. Once again the winch rope came down, once again men were pulled up to safety in the belly of the aircraft. All except one.

'What's gone wrong now?' I asked.

'The winch rope must have jammed,' said Slim.

Swinging on the end of the rope a man was indeed suspended in mid-air. What were they going to do now? Like the Grand Old Duke of York with his men halfway up the hill, he was neither up nor down.

'What time's your hair appointment?' said Slim.

I looked at the clock. 'I've got to be there in five minutes.'

Five minutes, I had to go, didn't have time to wait and see what happened next. Slim was going to Lerwick to fetch building materials and was going to drive me down to the village, promising to pick me up on his return.

'Come on,' I said. 'Put your coat on.'

When I arrived at Lillian's cosy caravan-cum-salon I was able to see Quendale Bay from a different angle.

'Have you seen what's happening out in the bay?' I asked.

'No. What's that?'

The view from the window of Lillian's caravan took in the wide sweep of the bay, the windswept headland beyond and the imposing nine hundred foot high hill of rock called Fitful Head. We looked out of the window and could see that the tug was still on fire, though to me the smoke seemed rather less and the tiny figure of a man still on board was visible. The tug had also stopped circling and had resumed a forward direction. One disaster appeared to have been averted.

The chair that customers sat in to have their hair dressed faced the window overlooking the bay. For two hours that morning, while Lillian cut and permed my hair, tortured my head with curlers pulled tight and speared into place, I was able to continue watching as men fought to get the runaway rig under control again. By lunchtime they had succeeded to get a tow rope attached and with both tugs in working order the rig's journey to disaster had been stopped. Slowly the little cavalcade began to make progress out of the bay.

Next they would have to navigate their way round the southern tip of Shetland which would bring them into contact with the 'Roost', off Sumburgh head. The Roost is the name given to the waters there. It's the meeting place of the North Sea and the Atlantic, where tides converge and do battle, cause turmoil and churn the sea into a seething, boiling mass of water.

While I alternated between the chair and the kitchen sink, where Lillian rinsed my hair free of odd substances, and while I sat for varying amounts of time with my head swathed in plastic, there was a constant coming and going of people.

The postman arrived with letters, sat in the chair and was deftly given a short back and sides. A toddler, brought in by his mother, protested loudly as he was divested of his baby curls. Another lady was given a shampoo and set and every time the door was opened a cat either came in or went out.

'How many cats do you have Lillian?' I said.

She laughed. 'I don't know. Sometimes my ones bring their friends home and cats do seem to multiply, don't they?'

In view of this last remark I made a mental note to take Thomas, as soon as he was old enough, to the vet for the necessary operation.

'Do you have spy glasses Millie?'

'Spy glasses?'

'Yes. You know, a pair of binoculars.'

'Oh, yes. We were watching the rig through them this morning.'

'Everybody in Shetland has them,' said Lillian. 'They're fine things. You can look out and see what your neighbour's doing.' She had the grace to chuckle here. 'Then you see the glint of the sun on glass and you know that your neighbour's watching you too.'

So that's how the grape vine works.

The morning passed quickly and soon the curlers were taken out and my hair brushed and styled. Gone were the long wispy locks and in their place were curls, short and close to the head. It felt good. The wind could not play havoc with me now. I had hardly settled my bill and put my coat on when there was a knock on the door and Slim was there to pick me up.

As the year progressed and the hours of daylight grew longer we were able to spend more time at Yawfield but were handicapped by only having one form of transport. It was sometimes inconvenient for me to use the Volkswagen when Slim really needed it, so he bought a small Renault 4 van for me. It was a very handy vehicle. A small section across the top of the back door could be removed, ideal ventilation when moving animals, it also made it easy to load and transport long lengths of timber. As well as being economical it was a pleasure to drive.

We were on our way home from the croft one day when Slim said something that I really ought to have seen coming.

'I think we ought to move up to the croft, Millie. We'd get on faster.'

'And what do you propose we live in?' I asked. 'A tent?'

'Silly girl. We could have a couple of caravans.'

My heart sank. I had lived in a caravan once and hated the lack of space, condensation and having to play general post with the furniture when I wanted to go to bed.

'You've got to agree that it's a good idea,' he went on. 'I would be able to do an odd hour here and there, the tools would all be at hand and we wouldn't have to load the van every time we wanted to do some work. Look at the time we'd save.'

He was right of course, but all the same I protested loudly, making my objections clear. Needless to say I was over-ruled and had to agree. Once Slim decided on a course of action he wasted no time in carrying it out and it was only a couple of days later that he came home and told me he'd found our first caravan.

Caravan number one was quite respectable, rather old but in good condition. There was one main room with a double bed that folded up into a cupboard in the wall, a single bed served as a settee in the daytime. There was a tiny solid fuel stove in this room. The kitchen was minute, a tiny room, opening off it, was a cubicle containing a single bunk.

We bought the caravan and towed it to Yawfield and with much pushing and pulling it was manoeuvred into position, jacked up and made level. We decided to enlarge the kitchen by removing the little room behind it and when it was done there was room for my gas cooker and fridge as well as a table and a couple of chairs. We now had living accommodation. All we needed now was another caravan in which to store our furniture.

Caravan number two had been abandoned in the middle of a field at the top of a hill. At some time it had been used as accommodation for some casual workers and when we went to inspect it, it was obvious that a woman's touch had definitely been lacking. The kitchen department was veneered with a layer of grease. Odd cups and plates were embalmed with the remains of food long since congealed and unrecognisable. Various articles of clothing lay abandoned on the beds. I groaned. Housework is not my favourite way of killing time, I do not much like clearing up my family's mess and I certainly do not like clearing up after strangers. Still, apart from the fact that one end of it had been used as a target by some boys with an air gun and was peppered with holes, the framework of the caravan was sound and that was the main consideration. I would have to buckle down with soap, water and disinfectant and make the inside habitable again.

'If we buy it, how are we going to get this one home?' I asked.

'I'll borrow somebody's tractor.'

The caravan was a newer model than the first and was not designed to be towed behind a vehicle. The wheels were small and only intended as a means of jockeying it into position when it had reached its final destination. Ones like this were usually transported on a low loader but any thought of a low loader negotiating the track to Yawfield was out of the question.

The initiative that certain Naval personnel seem to be endowed with came to the rescue. Taking the original roadworthy wheels off caravan number one, Slim drilled holes in them to match the studs on the hubs of number two. The small wheels were removed and the transport wheels fitted. Holes had to be cut in the floor inside to accommodate the larger wheels, and new wheel arches made. This done, we were ready to roll and the caravan was hitched up to the borrowed tractor. I was detailed to go ahead and to wait at intervals until Slim and the caravan came in sight.

The holes that Slim had drilled to fit the new transport wheels were not quite right. The hub of one was off centre which gave the caravan a definite list to port and also caused it to move with the unsteady gait of a drunken sailor. While it travelled on the highway all went well, but the mile and a half of rough track from Ireland to Yawfield was too much. The track was pitted with holes and when the caravan finally lurched into a particularly deep hole it gave up the ghost and buried its nose in the mud. But Slim was not to be outdone, next day he made a new draw bar of wood, fitted it and towed the caravan to its final resting place.

Both of the vans had been placed along the side and back of a stone built shed on the only level piece of land at the croft. All that had to be done now was to get the electricity connected and water laid on. Electricity was easy, there had been a supply to the house so it was not much trouble to connect it to the caravan. When it came to water it was a job we had to do ourselves and we didn't know whether we would be lucky or not.

'I suppose I shall have to carry a pitcher and go to the well like they did in the old days,' I said.

I thought of the old clay pitcher that had belonged to my mother and which we had used to fetch our drinking water from a spring when I was a child. I still had the pitcher but didn't really think about using it again.

'We've got the well up at the top of the field, haven't we,' said Slim. 'All we've got to do is pipe the water down to the house, or the caravans I should say.'

'It's not very deep, there isn't much water in it.'

'But you know what Bobbie told you. It never ran dry and all the people on this side of the hill came to it for water.'

'Yes, but do you think that they used much water? After all they could have got water for washing clothes from the loch. Having to fetch and carry water is quite different to having a tap to turn on.'

'I know. But the fact that the well never used to run dry tells me that it's artesian. You know what that means don't you? It's fed from an underground source, it may even start on the hill the other side of the valley. If I use the right valves and things we'll never overcome the header tank I shall have to fit. Now, let's go and inspect the situation and make a list of the equipment I shall need.'

Slim had been an apprentice plumber before he joined the Navy and had taken it up again when he left the service so I was sure he knew what he was talking about.

The well we went to inspect was just inside the top gate to our property. It was covered by a few rotten boards and when they were removed we could see that the water was full of weeds. We knew that it was not deep and when Slim put his hand in to test the depth, beside finding that the water came no higher than his elbow, he found a small frog.

'That means the water is good,' he said. 'If it wasn't, the frog wouldn't be able to live in it.'

When the weeds had been pulled out and the water had cleared we could see that a spring bubbling up from the ground was the source. A topless and bottomless barrel had been set down over it and concrete poured round the outside to contain the water. Over the years the barrel had rotted away and only the impression of its shape was left in the concrete. The overflow from the well ran out in a steady stream. A ditch had been dug from the well to direct the water away down the hill and peter out somewhere below the house, but it didn't get that far for it seemed to be absorbed by the peaty soil and little of it got into the ditch.

'Before we do anything we have to have this water tested to see if it's fit to drink. Ring the council tomorrow Millie, and find out what we have to do.'

A time was agreed for the Environmental Health officer to visit Yawfield to take samples of the water. When he arrived at the croft a couple of days later he was clad all in green, trousers, shirt, jumper, wellies and mac. But when he smiled his cheeks swelled into little red apples. From a case he produced three small bottles which he proceeded to fill with well water. He asked us what we intended doing with the house and when we told him we were completely renovating it he was interested to take a look. I am sure he was of the opinion – as I'm sure were many others – that we were quite mad. 'My, you've taken on a lot,' was all he could say. He promised to let us know what the result of the analysis was as soon as possible.

Less than a week later we were told the water was excellent, the only thing it was short of was calcium, but that could be rectified by what we ate. We were delighted with the result as it meant we could go ahead with our plans to pipe the water to the house.

'First thing I'm going to do,' said Slim, 'is to box in the well. It would keep surface water out and the animals away from it. If we're going to drink it, better keep it clean.'

So he built a well house. It was constructed of blocks, had a wooden, felt covered roof and was boxed in with a door. Now it would not and could not be contaminated.

'I'll connect a length of pipe to the well, run it down the ditch and put a tank in the caravan. We can get it to the house later. Better measure how much hose we want.'

Slim strode off down the field measuring a yard with each stride. When he got to the bottom he turned to me.

'That's it. I know what I want now. We'll go to Lerwick tomorrow and in a couple of days you'll have a caravan with all mod cons, electric, gas and water.'

'What about a bath and toilet?'

'No trouble. You aren't very big or Michael either. You could get into a header tank I reckon and I prefer a shower anyway. Toilet? Nothing wrong with a thunder box for a month or two is there?'

A header tank is the one that goes in the roof of a house to hold the water supply for the hot water system and the non-drinking cold water. The one we had, measured about two foot by three and was approximately two foot six inches deep. 'Thunder bucket' is Naval terminology for the old-fashioned bucket lavatory that stood in a small shed at the bottom of the garden path.

There was a time when I used to think I would have made a good pioneer woman. In my teens my favourite films were Westerns, I fancied myself in a long skirt and a poke bonnet, riding a horse or driving a wagon. I would have been able to shoot a gun with the best of them. Until now I had never given a thought to the toilet arrangements of a wagon train but, faced with the sort of predicament that must have been their daily lot, I was glad I was living in the present day.

Once the necessary equipment had been bought, on our next day at the croft we set about the task of setting up our water supply. The coil of black plastic pipe was unrolled and laid down the field from the well to the caravan. Slim then fitted a galvanised iron pipe through the concrete wall of the well and connected it, with an elbow, to another pipe which went down to about two inches from the bottom of the water. The plastic pipe was fitted to the iron pipe on the outside. Now all we had to do was to get the water to syphon up through the inside pipe and travel down the field to the caravan. Easier said than done.

Turning the pipe, which had been pointing at the bottom of the well, up to face me, Slim gave me a jug.

'Now,' he said. 'I want you to stay here and pour water into the top of that pipe until I tell you to stop and turn the pipe down. Is that an OK?'

'That's an OK,' I said.

'I'm going down to the bottom to bleed the pipe.'

I stood there, my feet in the mud where the overflow had saturated the soil, and watched as Slim went down the hill. It was a glorious day and I hoped getting the water supply connected wasn't going to take too long, I had other things I wanted to do.

'Right, start pouring,' shouted Slim.

So I did. Jug after jug after jug. I poured gallon after gallon of water into the mouth of that pipe. It was like trying to fill a bottomless pit. From time to time Slim shouted 'stop pouring' and I thought it was done. But no, off I would have to go again, fill the jug, pour it into the pipe, listen to it gurgling away as I filled the jug again. Then, 'Stop. Turn the pipe down.' My heart leapt, we'd done it. I threw down the jug and quickly turned the pipe down into the water, turned and looked expectantly at Slim. But he only shook his head and told me to turn the pipe up and start pouring again.

From time to time bubbles popped out of the top of the pipe at me but apart from that nothing seemed to happen. I was beginning to think that mother's pitcher might come into its own after all. Irritated at our seeming lack of success Slim shouted at me and I shouted back. After much running up and down the hill by Slim, after being yelled at to do as I was told, after near success followed by failure... there it was.

'Turn the pipe down Millie, we have it.'

I threw away the jug and quickly turned the pipe down into the well then looked towards Slim. He was doing something with the end of the plastic pipe. Then his head came up and a huge grin spread across his face.

'I told you we could do it,' he yelled. 'We've got running water. Bags I turn the tap on first.' He got up and made for the caravan.

The beast. He was nearer to it than I and I knew he would get there first. But I had to try. I ran and leapt down the field but by the time I got into the caravan Slim was standing at the sink with his hand on the tap and a stream of pure clear water running from it.

'You turned it on, but I'm going to have first taste,' I said.

The water was tasteless as all good water should be, but clean and refreshing to the palate.

'Should go well with a drop of whisky,' said Slim.

CHAPTER SIX

With water on tap and electricity at the flick of a switch it was time to take up residence at the croft. We loaded our furniture into the Volkswagen, carried it to Yawfield and, along with boxes of books and other small items, stacked it in caravan number two. The kitchen in number one was fitted out, clothes stored in wardrobes and one or two pictures hung on the walls.

The outhouse, which was flanked by the caravans, was to serve as an outside toilet but first its roof needed to be repaired. That done, doors were fitted and a chemical toilet put in. Our bath, a water tank above which Slim had fitted a shower unit, hot water by an Ascot type heater, was in caravan number two.

When everything was complete we were ready to move so we handed over the keys to No 10, Thistle Court and started on our new life at Yawfield and the renovation of our house.

Rule number one when restoring a house as old and battered as ours, is to see that the roof doesn't leak. Our house hadn't been lived in for many years and the roof was far from watertight. It had probably been thatched at one time, but then it had been boarded in, a layer of canvas applied and the whole thing covered with tar. Roofs like this were quite common in Shetland.

When the house had been built the builders had had to dig into the side of the hill to level a site, so at the back, the eaves of the roof were level with the ground. Getting on to the roof here was easy but trying to locate the places where the rain gained access was not. The holes were like pinpricks and from outside, impossible to see. Looking up at the roof from the inside was like looking at a night sky liberally sprinkled with stars. Short of re-covering and re-tarring the whole roof it was going to be a difficult job to cover all the holes. But then I had a brainwave. Gathering a handful of rushes, I climbed up on the inside and pushed a spear of green through every twinkling hole I could see. Outside again it looked as though the roof was sprouting grass. Our job was easier now, with a bucket of hot tar and strips of cloth torn from a pair of Slim's old overalls we patched the roof until no more green spikes could be seen.

When the sun came north of the equator the days rapidly grew longer. As May progressed, the earth sprang to life, grass shed it's tired, worn out look as fresh green pushed up and our three acres of hillside started to take on a lush appearance.

'We shall have to get some sheep, Millie, or the grass will go to pot with nothing to eat it.'

Nanny had long since turned up her toes and Baby, as sheep are wont to do, succumbed to some nameless bug or virus and had just laid down and died.

'Where are we going to get them then, Slim?' I asked. 'Have we got to go to market?'

'No,' he said. 'I'll talk to somebody at work. Plenty of them are crofters and keep sheep. I'll get some off one of them.'

True to his word, Slim came home a couple of days later with four sheep in the back of the van. They were two sets of twins, one thick set and with short wool, the other fine boned with long wool. All four were very wild so we decided to tether them. We had been shown how to make a tether when we had the goat. One or two swivels are placed at intervals in a length of rope so that the rope turns and stays un-kinked in the process and the tethered animal doesn't get strangled. Well, that's the theory and it works as long as the swivels don't become snarled up with long grass.

Because the sheep were going to be little more than pets we thought they ought to have names. We called them Beauty, for the want of anything better, and Dracula because he had horns and an evil look in his eye. The other two were Flighty and Honey. Honey had the best fleece and Flighty was so stupid he used to run in circles if we so much as looked out of the door.

The most common affliction of sheep are worms, or perhaps I should say intestinal parasites, but whatever they're called they need to be got rid of if the sheep is to thrive. On my next trip to Lerwick I would have to pay a visit to the vet's office and obtain the necessary concoction to dose them with.

Lerwick was, and is, a spread out sort of town. I could never get in, do my shopping, and get out of it in less than two hours. Hurrying always to get my messages before the shops closed for lunch, on the day I was to get the sheep's medicine I left my visit to the vet's office until last.

I opened the door to his place and went in. In front of me were two men and a rather small, elderly lady. The two men were served and they left. The little lady took an empty bottle out of her basket and handed it to the vet.

'I'm needing something for the skitters Edwin,' she said.

'Ay,' said the vet. 'Sheep got worms have they?'

'They have.'

He took her bottle, disappeared through a door to a back room and returned with it filled with a white liquid. I wondered how many sheep she had to dose for the bottle wasn't all that big. He told her how much she owed him and when I heard what he said, I took a hasty look in my purse for I knew I'd spent nearly all of my money. I hoped I had enough left to pay for my needs. The little lady paid him and bade him goodbye.

'Now then,' said Edwin as he turned to me. 'What can I do for you?'

'I think I need what that lady just had,' I said, then hastily, 'but I only have four sheep.' The vet smiled at me. 'And I haven't got a bottle,' I added.

'Never mind, I expect I can find you one,' he said and once again disappeared into the back room. When he came back I was relieved to see that the bottle he was carrying was much smaller than the one he had filled for his other customer. He told me how much of the medicine I should give each animal.

'Have you got a gun?' he asked.

'I'm not going to shoot them,' I said.

'No, no.' He laughed. 'I mean a dosing gun.'

'Oh. No I haven't.'

'Well, I'll give you one of these.' He produced a syringe, without a needle, and told me that would do as well. I was now equipped with all I needed to attack the sheep's worms, so, 'look out fellers, here I come,' I thought.

After I had paid Edwin I was relieved to find I was still solvent. I had learned something that day though, next time I needed to worm the sheep I knew what to ask for. 'Something for the skitters please, Edwin.'

My visit to the vet's office reminded me that Thomas was growing fast and would soon need to be neutered. I delayed a while but when it could be put off no longer I rang to enquire when it could be done. Wednesday was the day set aside for operations. I was to take him in the morning and could pick him up again in the afternoon.

As the appointed day approached I wondered how Tom would take to travelling in the van. Shag liked nothing better than to be invited to go for a ride but Tom had only ridden in a motor once and that was as a kitten inside Slim's anorak. I wondered how he would react to a much longer journey. I didn't have a cat basket but thought he should be contained in some way if only for my own safety. I found a large cardboard box thinking that might do. I perforated it with holes so that he would get enough air and not suffocate but then thought he would surely try to force his way out, I'd have to cover it with something. The only thing that came to hand was an old pair of tights, splendid, for they stretched wonderfully and covered the box completely.

Wednesday morning and Tom was put in the box with the tights tied over the top. The box was put on the seat of the van beside me and Shag jumped in beside it. We were all aboard, so off we went.

For the first mile or two Tom sat in the box and wailed. Like a lost child he cried, his voice rising and falling piteously. I tried to console him.

'There, there,' I said. 'You'll be all right.'

Shag's eyes, already bulbous on account of his King Charles Spaniel genes, grew even more round. But still Tom wept. Shag didn't approve of the noise and moved himself into the farthest corner of the seat, as far away as possible from the banshee in the box. When I looked at him he returned my gaze with big brown eyes that held an expression of the utmost sorrow. Then the wailing subsided and came to a stop and I thought that Tom had at last resigned himself to this strange mode of transport.

For a while we rolled along as smooth as silk and I was happy to think that Tom had settled down. But then from the corner of my eye I saw a movement. I turned to look and there, rising from the box, was a beige nylon snake. It writhed and wreathed silently. Shag had glued himself even tighter into his corner, great big eyes almost popping out of his head.

Tom had squeezed himself out from the confines of string and sellotape, with which I had thought to secure him, and found himself in the cul-de-sac of one leg of the tights.

'Get down Tom.' I tried to push him back into the box but he would not go. His wriggling and writhing became more violent and suddenly, box, stocking clad cat and all went plummeting to the floor. This wouldn't do. I stopped the van and freed Tom from his bonds. Shag was delighted and greeted his friend with joy and as Tom seemed happy to be free I decided not to put him in the box again. For the rest of the journey he alternated between sitting beside Shag and climbing on to the back of my seat and draping himself round my shoulders. He was the perfect passenger and we arrived at the vet's without further incident. Once there I put him in the box again and handed him over. He would be ready for collection at three thirty I was told.

The rest of the morning was easy to occupy. I left Shag in the van and went into the town to buy a few things we needed and also to do some window shopping, a pleasure rarely indulged in. As it was Wednesday all the shops shut their doors at one o'clock so I was left with a further three hours to fill. I could have gone home and come back again but it seemed pointless to drive a fifty mile round journey just to be home for an hour or two at most.

I had brought some sandwiches and a flask of tea to have for my lunch. I shared the sandwiches with the dog then took him for a walk along the north road, stopped for a while to watch the shipping in the harbour, looked for seals but didn't see any. Back to the van then where Shag settled down to sleep while I read a book. Time dragged interminably and I thought of all the jobs I could be doing at home. At last the hands on my watch crept round to three and I could wait no longer.

When I walked into the vet's office I was greeted by his assistant, an Irish lad with a boyish face. Everything had gone without trouble, he said, and I could take my cat home. I settled the bill and was handed a box with the cat in. He looked very sleepy and dazed and did not respond when I stroked his head.

'He'll still be feeling the effects of the anaesthetic,' said the lad. 'But he'll be OK.'

Tom was sitting on a white jumper which I did not recognise and the box seemed different too. But it was Tom in the box, I was sure, his markings were correct, a white bib under his chin.

'I don't really want that jumper,' I said. The lad only smiled and said that he didn't want it either so I carried the box out to the van and put it on the seat beside the dog. I looked in at the unusually docile cat.

'Never mind Tom, you'll soon be all right again.' I stroked him, then picked him up for a cuddle. I held him out towards Shag who leaned forward to rub noses.

'Look. Here's your old friend waiting for you,' I said.

In one split second the sleepy cat in my hands exploded into a spitting, screaming devil. It leapt out of my hands, raced up the windscreen, flew upside down across the roof of the cab. It ran like quicksilver round my feet, swarmed up the door and along the back of the seats. Up, down and around he went like a mini-tornado. I sat there transfixed. Shag cowered in his corner, his eyes following every move.

'My God, what have they done to you Tom?' I cried. This was not the cat I knew. What had happened to make such a change in his personality?

Tap, tap, tap. And again, tap, tap, tap. I turned to the window and there saw the vet's assistant, a sheepish grin on his face. He mouthed, 'You've got the wrong cat,' and pointed to a box he was holding under his arm. So that was it.

Somehow I managed to catch the imposter in mid-flight and shove him back in his box, handed him over with a sigh of relief and gratefully received my own cat in exchange. The right cat at my side welcomed the advances of the dog, purred loudly and rubbed himself against Shag's enquiring nose, then climbed on to my lap. His actions told us, in more ways than words could have, that he was very pleased to see us again.

As with fruit, the price of vegetables in the shops amazed me. I had always had a vegetable garden and decided I would make one at Yawfield. At the back of the house was an area which was walled off from the rest of the field. Mimie told me it was what was called the kale yard. A variety of cabbage would have been grown there as winter feed for the animals and the family. Potatoes, carrots and swede would have been grown there too. It was too big an area to dig with a spade so I thought I might find someone who would be willing to plough it for me. But I was not thinking right, most crofters had full time jobs and with a croft to look after as well, time for them was at a premium. I drew a blank.

To solve the problem we bought a garden rotovator. After I had learned how to get it going and use it I drove it into what was to be my garden. I slipped it into gear and made a start. The ground was hard and the tines did little more than break the surface. I plodded on, the rotovator pecking at the turf. At the end of a couple of hours I had only covered an area about twenty yards by ten. With my ears buzzing from the sound of the engine and my arms aching from the vibrations of the machine I decided to call it a day.

Next day I attacked the garden plot again. This time the tines dug deeper into the earth, but there was an awful lot of chewed up turf mixed in with the soil.

For days and days afterwards I raked the dried turf and weeds into piles and made bonfires with them. With my machine I dug deeper in the earth, raked again and cleaned the soil of weeds until at last I was satisfied that my plot was ready for planting. The soil was rich and black and I was hopeful of producing a crop of good fresh vegetables for the family.

I was given a few boxes of seed potatoes and bought a few more. When they were all planted half my plot was filled. I had sown broad beans, peas, carrots, onions and swede in the rest. Happy to have accomplished this much I left the garden to its own devices while I directed my energies elsewhere.

After a week or so of housework, being a plumber's mate, hod carrier and builder's labourer I went back to my garden to see how it was getting on. The leaves of the potatoes were showing and there were wavy green lines indicating where I had put the smaller seeds. Weeds were growing too, it was time to hoe.

I was surprised at how quickly the things I'd planted had started into growth, back home in the south they would have taken several days more. I concluded that the rich earth at Yawfield was responsible. The hoeing done, once again I left the garden in the capable hands of Mother Nature.

Mother Nature may be capable but she also plays tricks on the unwary. At the end of another week spent moving rocks and helping to mix and lay cement I went to visit my garden again. I was aghast, couldn't believe what I saw. Everything had grown a foot in height. Not only the potatoes, peas and beans, but the weeds too. The whole plot was a mass of green. Chickweed flourished and grew rampant between the rows. Mother Nature had run riot while my back was turned.

Every day from then on I stole what time I could to weed my garden. I complained to Slim about the swiftness of growth, but all he said was, 'What d'you expect, there's almost twenty four hours of daylight now. It's a short season, the plants have to grow while they can. They don't stop to sleep like you.'

Summer passed swiftly. Thomas, who showed no sign of resentment at being deprived of his maleness, proceeded to grow into a big, beautiful cat. He was as faithful as a dog and would come galloping up the field to greet us if we had been absent for the day. He was a great hunter and often caught rabbits as big as himself. In no time at all there was a wide area round the house on which no rabbit dared even put foot let alone dig a hole and set up house.

Shag, though he looked like a collie in his markings, had no sense at all when it came to sheep. I had threatened him with instant death if he touch one strand of wool on Baby's head, and, sensible dog that he was, he took great heed of my words.

Slim had been right when he persuaded me to take a job. As well as lifting my spirits it had given a boost to my personal finances. With money in the bank I could now afford to buy a calf. I knew that Andrew Manson, who worked at the airport as well as being a crofter, was going to buy a batch of weaned calves at the market in Lerwick. I thought to ask him if he would get one for me.

'Andrew,' I said when he next came into the canteen. 'I hear you're going to buy some calves.'

'That's right,' he said.

'Could I buy one of them off you?'

'You could.'

'And can I choose which one I want?'

'Ay.'

'Right then. Let me know when you've got them, OK?'

'Ay.'

Never had a deal been so easy to arrange. That evening I bullied Slim into helping me prepare a section of one of the outhouses on which the roof was reasonably sound. The hay rack was cleaned out, the door examined to make sure it was secure, then a layer of litter put on the floor. When we were finished we patted ourselves on the back and said we had a good calf house. Now all we had to do was to wait until Andrew had brought his purchases home from the sales.

Each day I scanned the queue of workers looking for their dinner but there was no sign of Andrew. I knew he had bought calves because Mimie told me that the ones in a field in front of her house belonged to him. They had bawled all night, she said. Wondering if there was some reason why he was off work I picked up the phone and rang his home. His father answered my call.

'I haven't seen Andrew at work,' I said. 'Is he ill?'

'No. He's had a day or two off.'

'Oh. I asked him if he'd get me a calf,' I said. 'Do you know if he did?'

'Oh yes,' said Andrew's dad. 'It's the little black one. That's the one he said he'd got for you.'

'Thank you,' I said. 'I'll see Andrew when he's back at work then.'

So much for being able to choose my own animal. Did he think I didn't know one end of a calf from the other? The next time I saw him I asked if he'd been successful at the sales.

'Ay,' he replied.

'So where are they then?'

'They're in the field at Robin's Brae.'

'When can I come and choose mine?'

'When would you like?'

'How about after lunch? We close for an hour then.'

'OK. I'll see you there.'

Andrew hadn't told me that he'd already decided which calf was to be mine so I invited Alison and Maria to come with me and listen while I pulled his leg. They were only too willing so we cleared up as fast as we could, piled into my van and drove to Robin's Brae.

Andrew was already there with his friend Ronald. When they saw us they started to walk away across the field so the three of us fell in behind. Calves were dotted about in bunches. Among the first group was a nice blue heifer.

'Wait Andrew,' I called out. 'I'll have that one.' I pointed at the heifer.

'No, no. Not that one.'

'What d'you mean? Not that one. You said I could have my pick.'

'Ay, ay. But not that one.'

The two men strode on with the three of us women strung out behind. Alison and I were equipped with sensible footwear but Maria was totally ill shod and made heavy work of the rough ground. We came abreast of another group of calves and I called to Andrew that I would like the red one in the middle.

'No, no,' he said.

'Why not?' But he only shook his head.

The calves we were looking at were obviously not friends for they were strung apart in twos and threes in all corners of the field. At each lot I shouted after Andrew that I would like one of them and every time the answer, 'No, no,' came back. At last we came to a small black Hereford steer standing on its own.

The five of us stood in a semi-circle and looked at it.

'What's this then Andrew?' I said. 'I don't think much of that. Whatever made you buy it?'

There was nothing wrong with the calf, in fact it was a good one and one I would have bid for if I had been at market.

'That's yours,' said Andrew.

'Mine? I thought you promised I could take my pick.'

'And if I had you would have taken the best, wouldn't you?'

'Well, thank you for that. But I knew all along which one you had bought for me. I phoned to see where you were when I didn't see you at work and your father told me. Still, it's not bad. I'll take it.'

We shook hands and the deal was done.

Slim had promised to pick up the calf in the Volkswagen. It was quite big enough to hold a four-month-old calf with room to spare, but the dear thing had been hauled away from its mother, had never yet been confined, and didn't like it. The noise and the sensation of being on a moving platform, set its adrenalin pumping and all it wanted to do was escape. The glass in the small window of the partition that divided the cab from the container had been broken and all that remained was a hole. Daylight shone through it and on the part of the road where to the left was a sheer drop to the sea, the calf decided it wanted to join Slim in the driving seat.

It lunged at the only escape route it could see and, its head stuck firmly in the hole, bawled loudly in Slim's ear. Slim's remarks are not repeatable here if his report to me it to be believed, but he stopped the van, admonished the calf severely for its unseemly behaviour, tied it more securely and continued on the journey. They arrived home safely and with the calf installed in the barn and sheep in the meadow I was beginning to feel like a real farmer.

September is the time of the Autumn Equinox. Though the wind blows most of the time in Shetland, Bobbie Smith had warned us that it blew more fiercely in September and we could be sure we would have gales. We'd have to see that everything was fastened properly otherwise it was in danger of being blown away.

"High winds and rain in all areas."

The disembodied voice of the radio announcer churned out the words that I had so often heard before. I had come to hate the wind and rain that made up so much of the weather. In rough weather, having to open and close the three gates that barred our way on the track to Ireland was enough to destroy any attempt to look good. The winds would blast me and the rain splatter me so that I frequently arrived at my destination looking rather the worse for wear. "Like the wreck of the Hesperus," my mother would have said.

On this particular day the wind had buffeted much as usual but had been little more than playful. The forecast could not be ignored however. I thought about our caravans and wondered if they would stand the test if the weather became severe. They were old and inclined to rattle if the wind became boisterous.

'Hi Mum. Bobbie says we're in for a big blow.' Michael was home from school.

'Oh, come on. We've had gales before. It won't be that bad.'

Who was I trying to kid? Last year we'd been living in a house. Things were rather different now. We were living in a couple of rattling old caravans on the side of a windy hill. We'd better do the right thing and prepare for the worst.

Michael, now twelve years old was becoming quite helpful and together we went round the buildings to try to make things secure. We piled rocks on anything that might get blown away and tied down what we couldn't move. As we worked we became aware that the wind was rising in strength.

'Listen Mum, there's the phone.' Slim was calling from the airport.

'Batten the hatches Millie. Tie everything down. The Met Office says we're getting the tail end of a hurricane so it's going to be a rough night. I'll be home in about an hour.'

CHAPTER SEVEN

It was getting dark and with darkness came squalls of rain. Inside the caravan all was snug and warm. A fire burned in the little iron stove and a pot of stew on the cooker in the kitchen gave out comforting smells. Thomas sat in front of the fire and purred loudly but Shag, always nervous, looked at me with fear in his eyes.

'Don't worry old chap,' I said as I gave him a pat on the head. But as I looked at him I thought how dogs were said to be able to see ghosts and had a sort of sixth sense for all sorts of things, so I followed it up with, 'But don't look at me like that, OK?'

With one ear cocked to listen to the wind I went about the job of getting a meal ready for Slim when he came home from work. As I listened I thought the gusts of wind were getting stronger, but then they would lessen and I would breathe easy and think I was getting wound up over nothing.

Suddenly the wind gave a scream and the caravan shook as though in fright. Its thin walls flexed and a black wooden elephant flew off its shelf and hit me on the head. Funny, I thought they were supposed to be lucky. The elephant was quickly followed by another ornament, but this time I was not in the firing line. Michael thought it was great fun... but then, he would.

I was beginning to feel uneasy and worried for the safety of my little home and wished that Slim was home already. Suddenly, crash, bang. The door flew open. Thomas disappeared beneath a chair and Shag ran to hide in a corner, I jumped as though I'd been shot but Michael only laughed. It was Slim, filling the doorway, smiling and unruffled even though the gale was snarling at his heels.

The storm grew steadily in strength. Violent gusts shook and rattled the caravan. Cupboard doors flew open spilling their contents on the floor. Books cascaded off shelves and pictures chattered on the walls. In the kitchen my cooker was doing a samba across the floor. I grew more and more afraid that at any moment the caravan, with us and everything in it, would be turned turtle. My nerves were at screaming pitch.

'I'm not going to stay in this death trap a moment longer,' I said.

'So what are you going to do?' asked Slim.

'I'm going to sleep in the house.'

Though the roof of the house still leaked in places the walls were thick and unmoveable. I thought it would be safer there so that was where I was going.

'Are you coming with me Michael?'

The reply was a definite, 'Yes.' Fun had disappeared.

From our furniture store we took sun beds, pillows and sleeping bags. Slim helped us carry them into the house where we set them up. All the time the wind grew stronger and I feared for our safety. When Michael was tucked up I went back to the house to fetch the cat and the dog.

'I'm going to stay here,' Slim announced. 'No gale is going to move me.'

'Well, rather you than I,' I said and out I went into the storm. The wind screamed at me and pushed me about. The rain slapped and stung my face. In fear and anger I faced it, raised my fists and screamed back.

'Go away. Go away.'

The inside of the house was comparatively calm even though the wind howled down the chimney, whistled through every nook and cranny, and bumped and banged about the walls, but they were thick and built of granite, made to withstand the weather. I knew that the timbers holding up the roof were sound so I prayed that their covering would not be tempted to part company with them.

Shag and Thomas huddled together on an old chair. Michael was soon asleep but I lay there listening to the gale. Rain dripped through holes in the roof that we had missed, but we had put sheets of plastic DPC over our beds to keep us dry. I had found a candle, stuck it with molten wax to a saucer and stood it on the floor beside my bed where it flickered in the draught. It was a feeble light and small comfort but infinitely preferable to utter darkness.

Unable to sleep I lay there listening to the tumult going on outside. Demonic shrieks were followed by moans and groans. The door shook as though rattled by an unseen hand. It was as though some giant was frustrated at failing to get at us. I wondered if Slim was all right and at the same time wondered why I let him talk me into coming to this place. What on earth was I doing here?

As the night wore on I wondered how much longer the storm would last. From time to time the wind abated but each lull was followed by a renewed and frenzied attack. I noted how it imperceptibly shifted its quarter and as it did its strength seemed to grow fractionally less. The candle guttered to extinction in a pool of molten wax, but it mattered not, the storm was subsiding. I relaxed my vigilance and fell into a welcome sleep.

'Mum, Mum. Wake up. It's morning and the storm's gone.'

I opened my eyes to see daylight through the window. Shag bounded over to lick my face and Thomas jumped on to my chest. Michael was already out of bed and getting into his clothes.

'Where are you off to in such a hurry?' I asked.

'I want to see if there's any damage.'

Damage? I wondered if Slim was all right. I tumbled out of bed and scrabbled into my clothes. 'Wait for me,' I yelled, but he was gone.

Outside, everything was still, not the calm before the storm but perhaps a sort of apology for a wicked night. The caravans were still there, wonders would never cease, and inside Slim was making tea. It was the best I ever tasted.

'What sort of night did you have?' I asked him.

'It was great, like being back on board ship. I used to sleep under the flight deck and you could hear the planes landing. It was just like that. I thought I was back in the Navy.'

I might have guessed. Nothing much ruffles Slim. We had some breakfast then and afterwards went out to have a look around. Nothing serious had happened to our property but the grass, that the day before had been green, was now black. I wondered why and got down to have a closer look. The force of the wind and the lashing rain had beaten it to a pulp. My gosh! What about my garden?

The sight that met my eyes was unbelievable. The broad beans that had been ready to pick now leaned drunkenly, stalks completely bare of pods and leaves. My green peas, also ready to pick, had been reduced to an unrecognisable, sodden mass. Swedes were naked balls, their leaves had been stripped off, one had even been blown out of the ground. Potato haulm lay black and bruised. The only survivors were the carrots and potatoes which were safely underground. Heigh ho, so much for gardening.

After the storm came a period of calm. We heard that a caravan had been blown over a cliff though luckily there had been no-one in it. On the most northerly island of Unst, the anemometer, a piece of equipment that measures the strength of the wind, had been blown away. Plastic buckets and bowls were found in the most unusual places and sheets of galvanised iron had been picked up and scattered like a pack of cards. We had been lucky, apart from the fact that my garden had been wrecked nothing else had suffered.

When the wind and rain came roaring in from the west they travelled unimpeded over the Atlantic, climbed the cliffs to rush across the peat banks and whistle down the hill behind us. But the men who had built our house all those years ago knew what they were doing and the house crouched there with its back to the westerlies like a ewe sheltering in the lee of a peat bank.

Work on the house continued. By now, the whole of the inside had been stripped and new concrete floors laid. Foundations had been dug for the bathroom extension. The Volkswagen van, which Slim had taken south for repairs had been brought back again and with it had come some new units for my kitchen. They would have to remain in their boxes for some time yet though. We were not ready for them.

Of our four sheep, the two males had been despatched to the deep freeze, leaving Honey and Beauty at home. It was time to think about getting a mate for them. Some friends who lived at Levenwick had two black ewes that they had asked us to look after for the winter and they also wanted them to be put to the ram. It was hardly worth buying one for that small number so we decided to ask a neighbour if it would be possible to hire the use of one of his. Willie Tait, who lived at Ireland, just at the end of our track, said we could get the use of his tup.

'But we don't put the ewes to him just yet,' he said. 'We don't want lambs before April, the weather's too bad.'

So I waited, and not wanting to be pushy, left it too long. When I finally phoned to ask when we should bring the ewes to the ram he said,

'You're too late. They've all gone to the hill.'

'Gone to the hill?' What the devil for, I thought.

'We put them to the hill with the ewes for the winter,' he said.

So that was it. 'Oh. So I'm too late then.'

'Ay. But I have a ram here.'

'You do? What's he like.'

'Ay, he's awfu' bony.'

Crumbs. What good was a bony old ram. My heart sank. I'd really messed up this time. Why had I waited so long.

'He's a fine fleece on him, grey, awfu' bony. He's a Shetland.'

He couldn't be bony if he had a good fleece. Then the penny dropped. It was not 'bony' that Willie was saying, but bonnie. The accent had floored me once again. I breathed a sigh of relief.

'Oh... that's good Willie. I'll come and see you on Saturday.'

If I wanted to see Willie Tait for anything I always went on a Saturday, for that was when Bella made bannocks.

The ram Willie offered me really was bonnie. His coat appeared to be grey but when it was parted, next to his body it was almost white, darkening along the length until the tips were nearly black. The fleece itself was wonderfully soft, typical of the native Shetland sheep. It was not a big animal and seemed not to be aggressive, a fact I was pleased to note seeing that he sported a fine pair of curling black horns. I thanked Willie for the loan of it, bundled it into the van and took it home. With a bit of luck, when spring came we would have lambs in the meadow to delight us with their antics.

With the approach of winter social life in the village of Bigton took on a new note. Dances were held and November was the time of the Reestit Mutton Supper. Mimie asked us if we were going.

'What is reestit mutton?' I asked.

'Before we had freezers when a sheep was killed some of the joints would be put into pickle – salt brine you know – then taken out and hung up to dry.' She pointed up at the pulley above the Rayburn. 'That's some up there.'

Hanging from the bars of the pulley were some dried and dessicated pieces of something I couldn't put a name to.

'Are you sure that's edible?' I said. 'I thought it was your secret weapon.'

'Of course it's edible,' she laughed. 'But you have to soak it in lots of water to get the salt out and then it has to be boiled. Makes a fine pot of soup.'

'I'll take your word for that,' I said.

'In the old days it was a mainstay,' said Mimie. 'It would keep for months and was the winter's supply of meat. I think a lot of people would have gone hungry if they hadn't any. I don't know what they'd have done without it.'

'So, is the supper an annual affair, and is there a dance afterwards?'

'Yea, there is. Will I get you some tickets?'

I agreed that she should, one for Michael too, for it was a family affair and lots of children would be there.

The weather was kind on the night of the supper and although the wind blew, as it always did, the rain held off and I managed to arrive at the hall without looking as though I'd been pulled through a hedge backwards. As we drove down through Ireland towards Bigton we could see the lights of the village hall twinkling in the dark. On all the roads round about were the beams of car headlights and all were pointing in the direction of the hall. It seemed that everybody in the neighbourhood was going to be there.

We parked the car and walked towards the entrance, standing about outside were several men. It was a cold night and I wondered why they were there.

'What are they doing Slim?'

'Sinking a few red cans before they go in. The hall hasn't got a drinks licence.'

Inside the hall the entire floor had been taken up by three lengths of trestle tables. Covered with white cloths, cutlery and glasses were set at each place and jugs of water and bottles of orange squash placed at intervals. Some people were already seated, Mimie and her family included. We found places near them and settled down to wait for the arrival of our supper.

As the hall filled with people the buzz of chatter grew louder. In summer days are long but the season is soon over and there is so much outside work to do that there is little time to socialise. When summer turns to winter and the days grow short it's time to catch up with all the news and gossip, time to relax and enjoy the company of friends and relations.

At last all the seats were filled and the chatter settled down to an expectant buzz. Now the supper was ready and being carried out of the kitchen by men and women with beaming faces, great dishes of meat, of potatoes and carrots, jugs of gravy. Soon the hall resounded to the clatter of knives and forks. Heads were bent over plates, the pleasure of eating almost more important than conversation.

'Have some more, have some more,' someone said as dishes were passed along. At last they were empty and the cutlery was laid aside, the first course had been disposed of. Quickly the helpers came along the rows and empty plates were whisked away, almost as quickly dishes of trifle were served and a cup and saucer provided for tea or coffee.

Across the table from me I watched as a man took a drink from his cup. How did he have tea when none of the rest of us had? Putting the cup to his lips he tipped it up and drained it. Then he put it under the table. Seeing that I was watching him he grinned and replaced the cup on its saucer. It was not tea he was drinking but a sly dram.

When the serious business of eating was over the arrival of coffee was the signal for conversation to come into its own again. I wondered what they were all talking about. The price of sheep, of turnips, of hay? How were the kids, who was having a baby, who got married or flitted? I listened, for I loved the Shetland accent, softer than Scottish and with many Nordic words. Not surprising really, for the islands once belonged to Norway and despite them now being classed as a county of Scotland, the ties with Norway are still very strong.

I was happy to sit there and listen but the second half of the evening was about to get under way. The band had arrived and were setting themselves up on the stage. Helpers came between the lines of chairs to take paper dishes and napkins and throw them into rubbish bags, others came with trays on which to stack cups and saucers. The tables were cleared and the long paper tablecloths whipped away. Men left their seats and went outside, presumably to 'sink' a few more red cans while the women went to the ladies room to primp their hair and powder their noses.

The activity now as the room was being cleared was almost frantic. A curtain above the stage was pulled back to reveal a storage area, a man appeared at the opening. Trestle tables were folded and handed up to him to put away. The floor was cleared and swept. Crystals were scattered on the boards to make a smooth surface for dancing feet. Children took advantage and ran and slid as though on ice.

And then the band began to play. Music set feet a tapping, inviting dancers on to the floor. Soon the room was filled with the sound of happy people. No smooching here, the dance was energetic, skirts flared as partners swung, then wove the patterns of jigs and reels. I sat beside Slim and watched. Slim was not a dancer and although I knew some of the dances, I didn't think anyone would come and ask me to dance with them.

An eightsome reel was announced and slowly the sets began to make up. It took a little while, some women being loth to take part for with an exuberant partner it could be somewhat hazardous. It was one dance I didn't know so I felt quite safe.

'Come on Millie, you'll do this with me.' It was Mimie's son Colin.

'Oh no I won't.'

'Yes, you will.'

'No, Colin.' I pulled back as he took my hand. 'I don't know how to do it.'

'It's quite easy, I'll tell you what to do.'

With Slim laughing at my dilemma and Colin pulling at my hand I was lost and I was dragged out of my seat in spite of continuing to protest. The sets were now complete, four couples to each. The music struck up and the dance began. I was pushed this way and pulled that, grabbed and held in a vice like grip, swung around until my feet left the floor, set down and with my head reeling, sent across the set to be met by another and twirled again. All the while there was laughter and beaming faces, hands clapping to the rhythm as other dancers swirled and twirled. And then it was over. Happy, laughing people mopped the perspiration from their brows and drifted away to sit down or seek a draught of cool air.

While the dancers regained their composure the band took a rest, refreshed themselves with cool drinks, flexed hard working fingers and sorted their music sheets. The interval was short and in no time at all the music began again and the dancing continued. A waltz, the Barn Dance, the Gay Gordons. A crofter pranced his wife through the polka with more zest than finesse. To my surprise I spotted Slim skipping his way through yet another reel.

The mood of the evening was of happiness, the hours flew away too fast and all too soon it was time to go home. Hats and coats were donned, scarves pulled up round the ears against the cold. Cars full of tired revellers pulled out of the car park and drove away into the night. The band packed their instruments into their vehicle and went home. The caretaker put out the lights and locked the door and once again the hall was silent and dark.

We left the village, drove through Ireland and turned on to the road that led over the hill to Yawfield. A lonely track, the holes in it were full of water from the winter rains. Some of the resulting puddles were very big, we drove round them but splashed through the small ones. Of necessity our progress was slow for the road was unfenced and sheep were liable to appear and disappear like wraiths in the gloom.

Christmas, and the children's party at the Clubhouse was the next major event. Slim was asked to stand in for Santa. I suppose he was the natural choice for he was rather large and over the years his beard had turned snowy white. As there was an absence of reindeer in Shetland, also sleighs, a pony and cart were to be used as substitutes. Garbed in red and with a totally unnecessary false beard Slim picked up his sack and got into his carriage. Someone said 'Gee-up,' and they were under way. Emerging from one of the hangars at the bottom of the hill they made a very pretty sight for the children waiting on the balcony of the Clubhouse. The pony trotted along quite happily until it got to the bottom of the hill, then it slowed to a walk which got slower and slower until it finally came to a halt. No amount of urging would get it going again.

'I think you're too heavy for it Slim,' someone said. 'You'd better get out and walk.' To a mighty cheer from the children Father Christmas got out of his carriage and with obvious relief the pony started to climb the hill again.

Slim is a sucker when it comes to children, loves them all. When at last he got to the party they engulfed him, all eager to see what Santa had for them.

With the sacks of presents by his side he sat himself down. Children ranged round him, some on the floor, some standing, some clinging to mother's skirts but all eagerly waiting to receive a gift from Father Christmas.

The older children were very blasé, thanked him for their present but made it plain they were only humouring the grown ups. Long since had the shades fallen from their eyes.

The little ones loved him, this was a fairy tale come true. But even at this tender age there were doubters and those more perceptive than others. One small, very blonde three year old boy, a neighbour's child, walked straight up to him, looked him in the eye and said, 'What you doin' under there Slim Vigor?'

Slim, trying hard not to laugh, in a very un-Santa like way replied, 'Git aht of it.'

And so the presents were distributed. Gradually the sacks emptied and the floor became lost under a sea of coloured paper. Ribbons and strings were hastily thrown aside, wrappings torn from boxes and bags to a rising crescendo of oohs and aahs and 'Look what I've got.'

At last the one remaining present was out of the sack and the children turned their attention away from Santa and to their toys and books. Duty done, Slim, sweating under a double beard and hot disguise went in search of a cup of tea and somewhere to disrobe before coming home.

Our Christmas festivities promised to be quiet, the season not being of such importance in Shetland as it is in England. Not being in a position to entertain visitors we put one or two decorations up in the caravan, cooked our Christmas dinner and gave one another presents. Mimie's oldest son, Laurence, had fixed us up with a second hand TV. Somehow the signal, which came from Bressay, was able to climb over the hill to give us a picture of sorts. We watched the Queen as she gave her speech, and full of chicken, Christmas pudding and cream, dozed through most of the rest of the evening's programmes.

Boxing day was quiet too, followed a similar pattern to Christmas day, as did the few days after. There was really nothing of great importance to do and it was mid-winter after all.

'Did you have a good Christmas?'

'Who is it?' whispered Slim as I answered the phone. 'It's Willie Leask,' I mouthed back.

'Yes, thank you Willie,' I said. 'We did.'

'You'll come and first foot with us.'

'Oh, will we? I don't know.' I turned to Slim. 'Willie wants us to go first footing with him, what d'you say?'

'Of course we will.'

I put the receiver back to my ear. 'Slim says thank you, we'd like to very much.'

'You'll stay a while wi' us then we'll all go along to Johnnie's house,' said Willie. 'Come along about eight o'clock.'

'Ok.'

And that was that, first footing it was then.

CHAPTER EIGHT

'Put the cat out Millie.'

'Why? He'll be all right here 'til we get back won't he? We won't be that late.'

'Want to bet? I doubt if we'll be home before morning. Put him out.'

Poor cat. I picked him up from where he lay, curled up and snug in front of the fire, carried him outside and, apologising for disturbing him, put him down. But he was only a cat after all and I knew he'd get into the barn and make himself comfortable on top of the hay.

'Come on Millie,' shouted Slim. 'What are you doing?'

'I'm here now,' I said as I got into the van beside him. Michael was sitting on a cushion in the back, all present and correct off we went down the track for another night out.

Willie and Elsie made us welcome, pushed plates of food and glasses of whisky into our hands. We were made comfortable in their sitting room and soon the conversation turned to Yawfield. Willie had been brought up there and it had been his home for many, many years.

'I was the only child in that little community,' he said. 'I knew all the people in the other houses, they were all old, and all of them were my friends.'

'Where did you go to school, Willie?' I asked.

'School? Don't talk to me about school. I had to trudge two and a half miles up hill and down dale to it, most of it rough terrain. I had to wear Wellingtons most of the time, but then most children did, due to the weather. I have no happy memories of school.'

'That's a shame. I'd have thought being with other kids would have been good for you.'

Willie laughed at this. 'Good for me?' he said. 'They were strange creatures, I knew nothing about other children. Remember, I had been growing up with adults. At school I often daydreamed about what was going on at home and how I wanted to be there. One incident I remember which you may or may not find amusing. In those days all our farmyard manure was taken to the fields and left in heaps, or roos, as we called them. I had been daydreaming in class, I was about seven or eight, and had not done the work that had been set me. I got a severe talking to culminating with the question, "What do you think will become of you if you don't learn your lessons?" To this I replied in Shetland dialect, I probably knew nothing else, "Weel, as lang as I kin coont da roos a muck apo da rigs ah'll be aricht." At that tender age I either had a pretty low ambition or a glib tongue.'

He then went on to tell us how, as he got older, he learned the work of the croft. He spoke about the horses they kept, how his father said that on their steep hillside it was as hard for the horse to drag the plough back up the hill as it was for it to plough a furrow down.

'And what do you think of Shetland?' he asked.

'Love it and hate it,' I said. 'I love the quietness, the peace, the lovely beaches and walking over the heather. But I hate the wind and the rain and not being able to get the things I want.'

'We all hate the wind and rain,' said Willie. 'Have another whisky.'

Elsie plied us with food, plates of reestit mutton, crackers and cheese. I stole a glance at the clock, nearly ten, another three hours and we would be home and in our beds.

'Come on then. We'll go to Johnnie's now.'

Willie got up, put on his hat, Elsie a coat, and all of us, Willie and Elsie, Marilyn and Edna, their daughters, Slim, Michael and I went out into the night and trooped a short distance along the road to Johnnie's house.

Johnnie Jamieson and Julia along with their two sons, Brian and Nigel and old Micha, Johnnie's dad, lived just a couple of houses away from Willie. When we walked into their kitchen it was fine and warm, something cooking in a pot on top of a Rayburn smelt good. Once again we were made most welcome and glasses of whisky poured for us. Soon we were invited to eat.

This time we sat at the table and were served with dishes of potato soup. Taatie soup, as Shetlanders call it, is in itself the basis of a hearty meal. Potatoes, carrots, onions and reestit mutton all went into a pot and were boiled together. Sometimes a handful of barley was thrown in. The result was more like stew and bore no relation to the somewhat indifferent soups dished up back home. The soup was followed by more reestit mutton but this time with vegetables and gravy. After this came a bowl of trifle. It was very late at night to be eating such a meal, I thought, indigestion was going to sit like a ton weight on my chest all night.

If the meal had been good the company was better. Time flew and almost before we knew it midnight was upon us and the New Year on the doorstep. Glasses were charged to toast it and as the clock struck the hour, glass chinked on glass, everyone wished everyone a happy and prosperous New Year and hugs and kisses were exchanged. We stayed a while longer but then Willie announced that it was time to go first footing. Out we trooped again en masse and with Willie in the lead we crossed the threshold of Ric Nickerson's house. Once again the bottle was tilted and whisky was poured in a glass for us. No pub measures these and not being much of a drinker I decided that enough was enough, New Year or not.

We'd welcomed the New Year at Johnnie's house, taken it into Ric's and after a while of talking of this and that it was time to go back to Willie and Elsie's place. The time, when we got there, was nearly one a.m. Shouldn't we be going home? Willie had fallen asleep in the chair and Elsie looked as though she would welcome her bed.

'Are you going on anywhere else?' she asked when we said it was time to go. 'Everyone goes to Lang Jim's at New Year.'

'We hardly know him,' we said.

'I don't think that matters,' said Elsie.

It was decided that to Lang Jim's we would go. We said goodbye to Elsie, thanking her for her hospitality and turned the van in the direction of Bigton. All thoughts of getting to bed were now abandoned, the tiredness peak had passed. Lights glowed in the windows of every house we passed along the way. We were not the only ones to be casting off the old for the new.

At Lang Jim's the front door stood wide open, windows too. Through them came the buzz of conversation, laughter and music. Walking in we were met by smiling friendly faces, some I knew, but most, not. Inevitably, despite my protestations, a glass of whisky was thrust upon me. The house seemed to be full to overflowing, Elsie was right, everybody did go to Lang Jim's at New Year but I found a seat at last. I thought that if no one else was getting tired at least Michael must be, but he too had found his second wind and, with a glass of coke in his hand, was deep in conversation with a school friend. I looked round for Slim, saw him animated and in his element. Most of the revellers were known to him, some of them he worked with, but he was a gregarious character and would quite happily strike up a conversation with a complete stranger.

As the hands of the clock crept round, two o'clock, three o'clock, four o'clock, I sagged. Drink had dulled my senses and tiredness was hanging on every limb. Would it be possible to stop Slim talking and get him to take us home?

'In a minute,' he said when I asked him if we could go. 'In a minute,' he said when I tugged at his elbow.

Then the man he was talking to said, 'Come down to my house. It's just across the valley from you.' And of course Slim said we would.

We left Lang Jim, his wife and friends, went out into the darkness and followed the stranger's car to what had been Brodie's house. Slim and his new acquaintance picked up their conversation right where they'd left off. Michael and I sat and waited for them to stop, drank coffee and watched as a grey dawn crept slowly across the sky. My eyes were heavy and the desire to creep into bed grew stronger by the second.

'It's no good, Slim,' I said. 'I just have to go home.'

'In a minute.'

'No. Not in a minute. Now. I'll take the van, Michael will come with me and you can walk home when you're ready.'

'All right then.'

So I drove home, Michael as glad to go as I. Back up the valley, skirting Bigton, turning right for Ireland. All was quiet now. Houses were shuttered and curtains drawn. We saw no-one, only sheep along the track, their coats spangled with the early morning mist. At last we closed the last of the gates behind us, trundled down the hill and brought the van to a halt outside the house. We decided that we'd well and truly welcomed the New Year but that all we wanted now was bed and sleep.

Slim walked home across the fields and climbed into bed mid-morning.

Another year was beginning and though January and February would bring many dark and dismal days, rain and wind and possibly snow and ice, we were on the run down to spring and thence to the days of Simmer Dim.

Living in the caravan was not as bad as I had anticipated. After the hurricane had thrown its fury at it, battered and shaken it and it had survived, I thought it was as safe as the rock of Gibraltar and when the day's work was done and the fire alight in the little iron stove it was comfortable and warm.

We did not venture far on winter nights, the unpredictable weather saw to that. Often the mist would come swirling in off the sea enveloping everything in a damp white shroud. A strange quietness would descend, broken now and then by the bleat of a sheep and the far off sound of waves breaking on the sands at Maywick.

Stepping out of the caravan on just such a night to fetch a forgotten article from the house I was startled by a strange noise.

Rrrrr Rrrrr Rrrrr Rrrrr.

It seemed to come from a little way off, then from above me.

Rrrrr Rrrrr Rrrrr Rrrrr. There it was again. It was difficult to pinpoint just where it was coming from. I didn't know what it was, I had never heard anything like it before. Unbidden thoughts of the little men, the Trows, sprang to mind and goose bumps raised themselves on my flesh. I made a hasty retreat back into the caravan.

'Slim,' I said. 'There's something strange outside.'

'Strange? What do you mean?'

Now that I was safe inside I felt a little foolish.

'There's a funny noise. I think it's coming from the sky.'

Slim laughed, but he got up from his chair and together we went outside to investigate. The mist still swirled about us, and though we couldn't see them, we could hear sheep cropping the grass somewhere near at hand. We stood and listened, waited for whatever it was to make the noise again. But all was still and all we could hear were the sheep and the sound of the sea.

'You must have imagined it Millie,' said Slim and turned to go back inside.

'No. Wait.' I hung on to his sleeve, made him stay. I strained my ears, hoping against hope it hadn't all been imagination when suddenly there it was, a whirring resonant sound.

Rrrrr Rrrrr Rrrrr Rrrrr.

'There, did you hear that?'

'That,' said Slim, 'is a snipe. Haven't you ever heard one before?'

'No, I haven't. It's a funny noise for a bird to make isn't it? It isn't singing. How does it do it?'

'They fly up and then make a vertical dive. Their tail feathers vibrate and that's what makes the noise.'

So, that was another snippet of information to store away in the old grey cells and now that the sound had been identified there was no need to stand outside in the cold any longer.

Coming from a part of the country where there seemed to be birds in profusion my first impression of Shetland bird life was that there were not many at all. How could there be? There were no trees, or at least very few, no hedgerows, no shrubs. Where would they make their nests? Where would they find food? I found out that not seeing the birds was because I didn't know where to look.

On the hill to the west of our house were the peat banks. The area was called the Ness of Ireland, covered with heather and a wiry sort of grass it was the common grazing for sheep. It was also the breeding ground for many birds, among them the skuas, curlews, whimbrels and oyster catchers. There were probably others.

Two types of skua made their nests among the heather, the great skua and the Arctic. When Slim rode his motorbike along the track it was not unusual for him to be attacked by them. They are very fierce birds and would dive bomb him fearlessly, even striking his crash helmet, until he was out of the area. But then he took a stick, long enough that when he pushed it down inside the back of his jacket it would protrude above the level of his helmet. From then on they never struck him.

We never went walking anywhere near the birds in the breeding season, but if the path we took was too close to them we always took a stick. Holding it vertically above our heads was enough to keep us safe from claws and beaks.

Skuas appear heavy and ponderous in flight when they are not hunting but the chase reveals how swift and skilful they can be. In my opinion the Arctic skua is the expert when it comes to the art of flying. Sometimes when I took the dog for a walk I would sit in the shelter of a plantie crub and watch them. They fly very fast, dive at terrific speeds, even zoom between the strands of a wire fence. I never once saw a feather misplaced though I often thought they'd come out on the other side like chips. Shag never tired of chasing birds though the skuas were not as much fun as the gulls. The gulls never touched him but the skuas dived on him and sent him rolling in the dirt, but he'd never give up and would run and run until I called him back to me. Then he would drop to the ground, red tongue lolling, gasping for breath, just waiting for me to tell him to go again.

The oyster catchers were my favourites. With their black and white plumage, long orange bills and pink legs they were very conspicuous. When they had chicks in the nest they would do their utmost to lure us away. They would run, one wing dragging and their beaks almost sticking in the ground. I always wondered if one of them would ever trip itself up. One day it happened and a bird executed a somersault before my very eyes. When their young were old enough they had flying lessons. Every day the family circuited our house and as they flew they uttered loud kleep kleeps. They were like day trippers, strung out in a line, talking at the tops of their voices. Perhaps they were only being taught recognition of their territory but whatever the reason for their route, it always made me smile to watch them go by. The place became very quiet when the youngsters grew up and left home.

That summer a pair of red throated divers came to nest and breed by the side of Vatster Loch. Unmistakable in flight, their rapid wing beats suggest that they are in a desperate hurry but it's their incessant quacking that really gives them away. But they also have a call that bubbles and yodels and carries clearly over the waters of the loch.

These were some of the birds that either lived or came to breed in Shetland and that I got to know. But birds of a different kind were on my mind. Now that we were living at the croft I thought it would be nice to keep a few hens so that we could have a few fresh eggs to eat. When I asked Mimie where I might get some she didn't know. The men who used to raise chickens had all got jobs 'on the oil'. Was there anyone who hadn't deserted their usual employment for work 'on the oil'? There was a shortage of bakers, so bread was imported from Scotland. There was not enough milk produced so that had to be imported too. Of course the huge increase in the population might be blamed for these shortages.

Unable to buy chickens I resorted to Yellow Pages to find a supplier. The nearest hatchery seemed to be at Easter Ross in Scotland. I thought that day olds would be my best bet, cheaper regarding purchase price and the inevitable cost of freight. I rang, hoping to place an order.

'Sorry dear,' said a female voice. 'No day olds available, but I can let you have some point of lay pullets.'

It was Hobson's choice so pullets it would have to be. I asked how much they were and then ordered half a dozen.

'I'll give you a ring when they're despatched,' said the female. 'Then you'll have to pay the freight when you collect them from the boat. OK?'

OK it was. Slim and I cleared a place in an outhouse to make a home for our hens and then all we had to do was wait. They'd surely be here in the next day or two. A week went by before the hatchery called.

'Sorry dear.' It was that female again. 'There's a rail strike going on here, we can't get them to the boat. We'll let you know when it's over and your pullets are despatched.'

Oh well. These things are sent to try us.

When the railway staff went back to work the dockers in Aberdeen came out.

'Sorry dear,' said the voice from the hatchery. If she says "sorry dear" once more I'm going to go down there and strangle her I said to Slim.

Days and days went by and then at last came the call we had been waiting for.

'Your chickens will be on tomorrow night's boat.'

Hooray. I felt like jumping up and down. It had only taken three weeks from the time I placed the order to notification of a delivery date.

Next day the hatchery called again.

'Sorry dear.' Oh, not again. I clenched my fists and ground my teeth. What could it be this time? 'There's a gale blowing. The boat isn't going to sail.'

'Which direction is the wind coming from?' I asked.

'From the south.'

'It must be coming in our direction then. Why don't you throw the birds in the air and let them fly here?'

'Ha. Ha. Very funny. Sorry dear.' Oh, there she goes again. 'The gale will blow itself out. You'll get your chickens soon.'

In fact the chickens arrived a couple of days later. I collected them from the freight shed at Lerwick and was shocked to discover that the cost to put each chicken on the boat was equal to the sum I had paid for them. Their passage had doubled their price. Still, they were here at last. At least I would not have to worry about the possibility of a fox killing them for there were none on Shetland, there were no snakes either. Hares and rabbits, hedgehogs and stoats along with rats and mice were the only wild things. Stoats would be the only threat to the hens, but we had seen none in our locality.

'I'm looking forward to having a fresh boiled egg,' said Slim. 'I like hens' eggs but I like ducks' eggs better.'

'Can't have ducks, we haven't got a pond.'

'I could dig out the ditch where the overflow comes from the well and make them a pond.'

'You do that then,' said I. 'You'd better or they might go toddling off down to the loch and we'd never see them again.'

'They'd come home.'

'They might if Henry didn't fancy a duck for his supper, think they were wild and shoot them.'

On his day off Slim dug the pond, lined it and together we stood and watched as it slowly filled with water.

As luck would have it, the *Shetland Times*, our local newspaper, carried an ad the following week which offered, among other things, some ducks for sale. I rang the number given and was answered by a voice with a strong Shetland accent.

'I see you have some ducks for sale,' I said.

'Oh yeh. I reared them myself. They're awfu' bony.'

Ha. I can't be caught out this time, I knew what she meant. But it seemed an odd sort of description for a duck.

'What are they like?'

'They're black and white.' Black and white ducks? The mind boggled.

'Black and white? What breed are they then?'

'They're collies.'

'Collies? I said ducks, not dogs.'

'Oooh. You mean da dukes. I tot du said dugs.'

Would I ever get my ear in tune to this way of speaking?

The ducks turned out to be Aylesbury's. I agreed to buy them and arranged to meet the vendor in Lerwick. She lived on the island of Bressay and said she would bring them across on the ferry the following morning, which was a Saturday. Next day, Michael and I set off in the little Renault van to collect our ducks.

We arrived with time to spare. At the place where the ferry docked we parked the van so that we could sit and watch as the boat came in. A squat sort of vessel, it purred back and forth across the sound carrying vehicles and passengers to and from the island. It was on its outward journey when we arrived. When it made its return we got out of the van to watch. As it neared the dock the noise of its engines changed as they were put in reverse to slow the vessel. A great gurgling and bubbling noise arose as the water churned and boiled and turned up all the muck from the bottom of the harbour, then with a clanking and rattling of chains the ferry was berthed and tied up.

As the ramp doors were lowered we could see there were no cars on board, only a small female figure stood on the deck. She wore an old sou'wester and an oilskin jacket and on the deck beside her lay two sacks. She picked them up and proceeded to walk down the ramp toward us. As there were no other passengers it was obvious this was the person we had come to meet. We had brought boxes to put the ducks in, but no, she said she didn't want the sacks, we could have them. The ducks, in the sacks, were put in the back of the van, the money was paid, the deal settled, we said 'Good bye,' and started for home.

Now ducks are not noted for being pleasantly aromatic, quite the reverse in fact. Michael and I had detected that the sacks they were in had previously contained fish meal. In the close confines of the van the combination of the two smells was pretty overpowering.

'Pooh,' said Michael and, 'Pooh,' said I. We wound the windows down, hoping that the fresh air would dilute the pong but all it did was to circle round the ducks in the fish meal sacks and waft the smell back under our noses.

'I can't stand this all the way home,' said I.

'Neither can I,' said Mike.

'D'you think it would help if we took off the top section of the back door?' I suggested.

'It might.'

As soon as we could we found a place to stop, hopped out and removed the section and hoped that by doing so the offending smell would drift up and away. No such luck. Hot ducks in fish meal sacks are not to be recommended as passengers. The only solution to our problem was for me to put my foot down hard and drive home with as much speed as safety would allow.

Our ducks, actually four ducks and a drake settled down quickly and soon started to produce eggs. Aylesbury ducks are a heavy breed and are bred for the table rather than for egg production, but these ducks were the exception to the rule. The eggs they laid were big and there were lots of them. I used them mainly in cooking as, although Slim liked them boiled or fried, Michael and I did not.

Although my garden had been reduced to ruin by the hurricane we decided to cultivate the entire area within the confines of the wall. I would not attempt to grow peas or beans again but we needed feed for our sheep and there would be enough room to grow swedes and cabbage as well as potatoes and other root vegetables for ourselves. We tried again to get the ground ploughed but without success, so the cultivator was brought into use once more. The ducks thought I was doing it all for their benefit and trailed along behind me seeking for and gobbling up worms and leather jackets and any other tasty morsel that came to the surface. Ploughing evokes a picture of a man with a horse yoked to the plough and a cloud of gulls circling them. It was not the picture I made. The cultivator was my horse and as I struggled to keep it on a straight and narrow path my cloud of gulls had dwindled into a handful of waddling, quacking ducks.

Lambing rarely starts before April as until then the weather can be wet and cold and it is not unusual for it to snow right up until the end of that month. That spring it was cold and wet so we brought our ewes into the barn at night so that they should have a warm dry bed if nothing else. They were soon to give birth and each day I stepped out before I'd had breakfast in case one or both had started without me. But each day I was disappointed. When, oh when, were we to hear the patter of tiny feet?

M. VIGOR

CHAPTER NINE

'I'm fed up with going out there of a morning to find that them sheep have produced nothing but a heap of muck. You go Michael.'

My eager anticipation of finding one, two or more lambs in the barn had cooled considerably when, day after day, there was nothing but two fat and very pregnant ewes to greet me. I knew nothing about helping sheep to give birth and hoped that they would do the job all by themselves.

I heard the door open and shut, was that Michael? There were no shouts of joy so I presumed that once again there was nothing to report.

'No luck then Mike,' I said when he came into the kitchen.

'Not unless you count a set of twins.'

'Twins? Why didn't you call me?'

'I had to see they were all right first, didn't I.'

'All right? What do you know about sheep and lambs?'

Michael was continually surprising me by what he knew. Where he picked it all up I don't know, but then he did spend a lot of time with Bobbie Smith and most of his friends' fathers were crofters.

He grinned at me. 'There's nothing to it Mum,' he said.

I went out to the barn to inspect the new arrivals. How tiny they were. I stood and watched as they struggled to their feet, staggered to their mother and sought her teats and the life giving milk. Why did she keep turning round? Why couldn't she stand still and let them get on with it? I chewed my nails until at last her babies had found what they were looking for, latched on and with tails twitching madly sucked up their breakfast.

The second ewe produced twins a couple of days later. We now had four lambs cavorting in the meadow. We brought them into the barn at night for the weather was still cold and wet. The lambs on the croft next to us were not so lucky. It was a sorry sight to see them with their backs humped up, it was so obvious they were cold and unhappy. But the Shetland breed of sheep are hardy and none of the lambs died.

Lambing went on around us well into May. Ewes were brought into fields near the croft house where it was easy to feed and keep an eye on them. Once the lambs were well grown they were destined to be put back on the common grazing and more or less left to fend for themselves.

As one sheep tends to look very much like another there had to be a way to identify them. Although to the meek hearted it may seem a cruel method the way this was done was to cut a piece out of the animal's ear. Each owner's mark was of a different pattern to other owners and the patterns, or lug-marks, were recorded in a book kept by the parish.

The next work with the sheep came round about August when the wool clip would be gathered. As the year progresses and the temperature rises the fleece on a Shetland sheep's back comes loose naturally and if not cut off would fall off by itself. In the old days it would be pulled off by hand, a process known as rooing. In an effort to improve the meat quality of the native sheep, rams of heavier breeds were introduced. One result of this was that the natural shedding of the wool was lost to some extent and shearing became a necessity.

I watched as my neighbours penned their sheep and set about harvesting their crop of wool. Some laid the sheep down, clipped one side, then rolled it over to clip the other. Some sat the sheep on its haunches and again clipped one side then the other. Not all shearers were good at their job, some sheep had holes cut in them, on others the evidence of uneven clipping showed in ridges of wool left on, like the furrows of a ploughed field. But it's easy to criticise, I had never held a pair of shears in my hand, so how was I going to manage when it was my turn to clip my sheep? Thank goodness there were only two.

Michael had become very knowledgeable about the way Shetland folk do things. 'I'll help you Mum,' he said. One day, after he had come home from school, we got out our new pair of shears, spread an old sheet on the ground which we hoped would help to keep the wool clean, caught one of the sheep and made a start.

'Lay it on its side,' said Mike.

I wrestled with it, and for a comparatively small animal was surprised how strong it was, but eventually I got it to lay down.

'Make a parting under its chin,' Michael said. 'Then clip away.'

Well that was easier said than done. Our sheep had never been shorn before and made it clear that she didn't approve of what we were doing to her now. She kicked. She struggled. She suddenly seemed to have more legs than the regulation four. I was having a hard time trying to keep her still let alone cut off any wool. Then Michael sat on her head. Oh, ever so gently, and for a while she lay quiet. I clipped as fast as I could, holding the shears in my right hand, pulling the skin taught with my left so that I would not cut chunks out of it. With one side done, we turned her over. She had become more resigned to the procedure now and didn't struggle so hard. Somehow we got the fleece off in one piece and with hands and clothes well greased with the lanolin that exuded from her skin and wool, we stepped back and let her go.

I have seen prettier sights. There was a tuft of wool sticking out from behind one ear, another on her bum, how could I have missed them? Still, I had managed to remove her fleece without puncturing her and there were very few furrows. I felt rather pleased with myself. But one animal was enough for now, the other would have to wait for another day.

The fleece we had removed from our sheep was fine and soft. A good length, about four to five inches. I had no idea what I was going to do with it but Michael said I should get a spinning wheel and learn how to spin.

'You could make some fine jumpers,' he said. 'The wool is free.'

"When in Rome do as the Romans" has always been my motto, so why not, after all what better place to learn to spin than in Shetland?

'Where can I get a spinning wheel Mimie?' I asked when next I saw her.

'Whatever do you want a wheel for?'

'I have fleece off my sheep and Mike suggested that I learn to spin so that I could make him a home grown jumper.'

Mimie smiled at that. 'They have spinneys in the shops in Lerwick,' she said. 'But they won't be cheap. All the old ones have been bought up and taken south to sell as antiques. Nobody much does any spinning these days. Just the demonstrators in the Town Hall in the summer.'

Her answer was not very encouraging. If I got a wheel who would teach me? Not Mimie. She did knit but mostly on a machine and not often by hand. Some months later, when on a visit to relatives in the south of England I saw a wheel in the window of a craft shop, went in and bought it and couldn't wait until I was back in Shetland to set it up.

At home the box containing my wheel was set on the floor of the sitting room. I opened it. The wheel was in sections and had to be assembled. Slim, Michael and I deciphered the instructions and put the pieces together. My wheel was in the Hebridean style and what most people think of when a spinning wheel is mentioned. I couldn't wait to try my hand at it.

A fleece will spin best when it is 'in oil' I was told. 'In oil' means when it is fresh from the sheep's back and the natural oils that help to make it reject moisture have not dried out. If it is too dry the wool is rough and will not run smoothly. Sometimes it is possible to spin straight from the fleece, that is, if it is a good length and not tangled. Normally the wool has to be carded to straighten the fibres first. Cards, or 'cairds' are flat boards, covered with hooked wire teeth and with a handle on the back. They are used in pairs. Fleece is laid on one and the other used to comb it and pull the fibres straight.

Not wanting to suffer offers of advice and unhelpful remarks from either of my menfolk when I first tried my hand at spinning I waited until they were both away from home, Slim at work and Michael at school. Only then would I have a go. I carded some wool and made it into rolags or sausage shapes. I was ready to begin.

With my foot on the treadle I set the wheel spinning. For a few times it went round and round, then suddenly it decided to go in the opposite direction. Obviously I would have to get the wheel running smoothly before I could start to spin a thread. After several abortive attempts it began to purr. Now was the time to connect the wool to the bobbin. One of the tips Mimie had given me was to tie a length of knitting wool to the bobbin first and the other end of it to the end of the rolag.

'It will give you time to get the wheel running before you start to spin,' she said.

So that was what I did. I treadled, the wheel turned and the end of the wool flew out of my hands, dived through the hole in the spindle and wound itself neatly round the bobbin. Try again. Try again. Try again. Each time the end of the wool disappeared like a frightened rabbit down its burrow. With each disappearing act my blood pressure rose another degree and my temper grew more frayed, but I was determined not to be beaten. I would get something spun before my menfolk came home that day.

After many false starts I managed to control the wheel so it didn't run so fast and I achieved a sort of success. Fibres wrapped themselves round each other and a yarn of sorts began to appear. The wheel was still running too fast and the threads were so tightly entwined that the resulting yarn, which actually resembled a coarse and lumpy rope, was strong enough to tie a bull, but a spun thread it was. I had successfully negotiated the first step on the road to being a spinner.

Our daily round at the croft was falling into some semblance of order. We had fenced our three acres into paddocks. The sheep were moved on to them in rotation. This was so that they would graze fresh pasture and the grass that they had been on could be rested thus hopefully avoiding a build up of parasites.

The garden was easier to manage now that I was not so ambitious in what I decided to grow. The hens gave us a plentiful supply of eggs and the ducks outperformed any ducks I had ever known. The drake however was a monster. Arrogant and bossy, he dominated his wives. A philanderer was he and not content with four females to mate with he decided to annex the hens. Ducks and drakes copulate in water which was bad news for the hens because he'd chase them, catch them, drag them to the pond and have his wicked way. Unfortunately, he'd stick their heads under water and drown them while he satisfied his lust. He disposed of two before we found out.

Our sheep, never intended as pets were doing fine. The lambs had grown well and we decided it was time for a couple of them to make the journey into the freezer. First though we had to catch them.

'It won't be difficult,' said Slim. 'We can corner them.'

Into the paddock we went, Slim, Michael, me and the dog. We walked slowly across the field, the sheep going before us. They reached the fence on the far side, grouped themselves in the corner and turned to face us. It was too easy. There were four sheep and we only wanted two. We crept closer. The sheep stood their ground and looked us in the eye.

'When I say go, grab 'em.' A pause. Then... 'GO,' shouted Slim... and... gone were the sheep. Like lightning they moved. Under and over our outstretched arms and between our legs. Self-preservation is a powerful instinct.

We straightened up and turned around. Our sheep were bobbing along towards the other side of the field.

'We'll get them this time,' muttered Slim. We didn't. A couple more times we trailed across the field and attempted to catch our lambs. Each time we were unsuccessful. Slim was determined not to be beaten so his next plan was that we should chase them until they got tired. Neither Michael nor I were hopeful that this new plan would succeed but we would try anything once.

We set off at a run, each of us with our sights on one particular sheep. Shag thought it was a great game and manfully brought up the rear by sticking close to my heels. I ran as fast as I could and just as it seemed that I was closing on my quarry I caught my toe on a rock that was sticking up out of the ground and fell flat on my face. I regained a sitting position and looked round to see Shag sitting beside me, red tongue lolling and a grin on his face. I resisted the urge to hit him and instead watched as Slim sped past, hot on the heels of his intended victim.

It looked as though the sheep was going to evade capture for it made a right turn and was gaining ground. Frustration made Slim roar and he threw the stick he was carrying at the sheep. His aim was true and the stick caught the sheep on the back of the head. It faltered momentarily and that was its undoing, for Slim did a very pretty flying rugby tackle and brought the animal to a halt.

'I thought I'd killed it,' he said later. 'It rolled its eyes up into its head until only the whites showed.'

'With an eighteen stone man landing on top of it I wouldn't have been surprised if you had,' I said.

Well, that was number one, we bundled it into the van, closed the doors on it and set off after number two. Michael was quick and had it cornered behind the house but we were too slow in going to help him. The sheep leapt for safety and hit Michael in the mouth with its head. Luckily the only damage was that a tooth was knocked slightly out of line but that action by the sheep sealed its fate. We were just about to set off after it again when Allen Sinclair came through the top gate.

'What arrrr you doing?' he asked. He was a great one for rolling his R's.

'We're trying to catch sheep.'

He could have laughed, but he didn't. He just joined in the chase and the errant animal was soon caught. We were all out of breath by this time so what else could we do but adjourn to the caravan to drink tea and eat cake.

'You should get yourrrrselves a dog,' said Allen.

'We already have a dog.'

'I mean a rrrreal dog. One that will worrrrk the sheep.'

'I don't think we have enough for that. After all, round up time is only two or three times a year.'

Allen smiled. 'You mean to say you're not going to get yourselves a flock?'

'I think we've already got enough to get on with,' said Slim, indicating the house. 'But we can't sit here talking, got work to do. I'll see you later Millie.'

After Slim and Allen had gone I thought about Allen's remark about getting a flock of sheep. There was no way we could have a flock on our three acres but wouldn't it be nice if we were able to get some more land sometime. I liked sheep. My uncle and a great uncle had both been shepherds. I began to wonder if my liking for sheep was sign of a vocation or a family weakness.

The opportunity to buy more land came earlier than I had expected or hoped for. The crofter whose sheep I had fed and helped shear owned the land bordering ours. One day he told us that he had decided to sell.

'We don't really want it do we?' said Slim.

'No. I suppose not. But...'

'But what?'

'It would be nice wouldn't it? We could get some more sheep.'

'Do you really want to tie yourself down with a flock of sheep?'

Good question. But now that I no longer worked at the airport and spent the days on my own at the croft I would have time to see to them. I told Slim that. 'And besides,' I said, 'BA said that we'd be here for twenty years at least, I could grow old looking after sheep.'

'OK then. We'll put in an offer.'

We made our offer then sat back to wait and hear if it had been successful. I was on tenterhooks, couldn't sleep for thinking about it but Slim just went to sleep as soon as his head hit the pillow and snored his way through the night. At last, after what seemed like an eternity, the news came and I was now the owner of twenty-nine acres of land plus hill rights. Owning a flock of sheep would no longer be a dream. But Shetland sheep are notorious for having no regard at all for fences, first we had to inspect them and see if any needed to be repaired.

Miles and miles of wire fences mark the boundaries of fields in Shetland. There were no hedges to provide shelter for the sheep against wind and rain, just strands of wire for the wind to whistle through.

When all the fences had been checked and found to be in good order we were ready to buy some more sheep. We could either go to market and bid for them or we could see what was available locally. We did neither. The grapevine had already sent out messages and one evening the telephone rang.

'Hallo. Is that Millie Vigor?'

'It is.'

'I believe you were wanting some sheep.'

'How did you know that?'

'Aaah, well. I have some broken mouth ewes that might suit you.'

'You have.'

Broken mouth ewes are sheep that have lost one or two teeth and need feeding to keep them going. But they are capable of producing a lamb and the lamb they give birth to can be the nucleus of a new flock.

'We shall be sorting them out tomorrow, if you come down about eleven o'clock we can fix you up.'

He'd told me where to find him and how much the sheep would cost. The deal sounded reasonable and next day after I'd done my morning tasks I got in the Volkswagen and drove off to the south end of the island.

Derek Black was a man most definitely larger than life, in fact he took up the space of two men. I found him, with his workmen, sorting out his sheep. From a pen of old ewes we picked out enough to fill the van, must have been twenty or more, they were crammed in like sardines. We shut the door on them and when I'd paid him we shook hands and I made for home.

I was now a shepherd. I was in business.

Word soon gets around and in no time Willie Leask was up along to see how we were getting on.

'I hear you've bought sheep,' he said.

'I have. Would you like to come and look them over?'

He would and we walked out to where they were.

'Hmm,' he said. 'Well, they won't be with you too long but it's a start.'

'That's what I thought. And it didn't break the bank to buy them.'

'You'll need a dog for them though,' said Willie. 'I have a couple of litters of pups at home. You'd better come and choose one.'

'How much?'

'I'm not wanting any money. Call in when you're passing.'

The next time I was on my way home from shopping I turned the car's nose towards Willie's house. Elsie answered the door to my knock.

'You've come to look at the pups,' she said.

'I am, if it's convenient.'

'Come in, come in,' she said and held the door wide.

A collie bitch lay on the floor in front of a Rayburn with her litter of puppies squirming round her. A fat little pup detached itself from her and came straight to me. It sat down and looked up at me. I bent down to stroke it. It's coat was soft, woolly and warm.

'I'll have this one,' I said.

'But you haven't looked at the others,' said Elsie.

'I don't need to. This one has chosen me.'

Poor Elsie. She had two litters of pups to show me, one here by the fire the other in an outhouse and I had settled on the first one I saw.

'You really ought to look at the others,' she said, and to please her I agreed. In the shed another collie bitch lay with half a dozen pups round about her. Elsie picked one or two of them up to show me, but she was wasting her time. There had been an instant rapport between me and the puppy that had come to look at me and I knew that none of the others would do. We went back into the kitchen, Elsie and I, and she agreed that the puppy would be saved for me and she would let me know when it was ready to leave its mother. About six weeks it would be, six weeks and I would be the owner of what Allen would call 'a rrrreal dog.'

CLIFT SOUND.

CHAPTER TEN

Summer, such as it was, was drawing to a close and winter was just over the horizon. Soon it would be time to harvest the potato crop. In October the schools would shut for a week and everybody in the family would go to the fields to help bring in the potatoes. Our potatoes had been dug and stored in the barn, carrots lifted too. But hey, other people had potatoes to lift and all hands were needed.

'I'll come and give you a hand,' I said to Bobbie Mullay.

'You don't need to do that.'

'If I had a rig of potatoes you'd come and help me wouldn't you? I've done taatie picking more times than I can remember so I'll come along, OK? Just give me a ring and let me know when.'

Such was the community spirit that on the day of Bobbie's potato harvest, all and sundry were there. A tractor, with a potato spinner on the back, went up and down the rows, pickers dived in after it had gone by and in no time at all the row was clean. Paper sacks that had once held sheep or chicken feed were filled with potatoes. Up and down went the tractor and by mid afternoon the rig of potatoes had all been picked up and bagged. Bobbie came to thank me for helping.

'There's a sack of taaties for you,' he said. 'Take them when you go.'

'That's very kind of you, but I wasn't looking for payment.'

'But everybody has a bag. You'd get one anywhere you went to pick.'

Well that was a bonus. I thanked him. He stooped and picked a potato out of one of the sacks. It was kidney shaped and had a purple skin.

'Have you had any of these before?' he asked me.

'No. I've never seen any like that. What are they?'

'They're called Ash. They go nicely with a bit of fish. Here, take some.'

He took a plastic bag out of his pocket, proceeded to fill it with enough potatoes for a meal then gave it to me.

People were drifting away from the field now so Bobbie and I joined them and walked over the newly dug earth toward the road. I got into my van, waved goodbye and drove away. My goodness, I thought, as I realised just how much my back was aching, it's a hot soak in the tub for me tonight.

'We'll have to get the roof slated before the winter sets in Millie. But I shall have to get some help to make it ready for them, it's something you can't do.'

We had already got the slates for the roof but the work with stripping off the old roof and recovering was not a job for me. How he found him I don't know but Slim contacted a man who lived on Bressay to come and help. Pete Watson didn't have any transport so one of us, usually me, had to go to meet him off the ferry and take him back for the last sailing at night. The last sailing was just after five in the evening and if he didn't catch it he would have to stay on the mainland overnight. All too often we left the croft at the very last minute and I would have to drive very fast to get to Lerwick in time. I fancy my driving technique improved considerably because of it, though I'm not at all sure if this feeling was shared by my passenger.

Afraid that the weather would deteriorate and catch us out, Slim listened to the radio all the time, and, being involved with aircraft at the airport made a point of getting reports from the Met Office. We had already made a start on re-slating the roof but, because the hours of daylight were getting less and less, he said it was going too slow. The next thing I knew was that he had got hold of some floodlights and set them up so that we could go on working long after dark. I had become hod carrier then, keeping him supplied with slates.

It was while standing at the foot of the ladder waiting to take the next bundle of slates to him that I noticed a light in the sky. We could see the glow from the flare stack at Sullom Voe on a dark night but this light was not from that direction. It was different too, not orange as the light from the stack but like a small wispy cloud and pale green. As I stared at it, trying to work out what it was the colour became more intense and the area it covered became larger. Other patches of colour started to appear, blue, red, orange. Then realisation dawned.

'Look Slim,' I shouted. 'It's the Northern Lights.'

All thought of work was now abandoned and we watched as the whole sky became filled with colour. Great shafts of red flared up from the horizon to the apex of the sky, brilliant blues and greens rolled beside them. Broad bands of colour flew across the heavens, vast sheets of orange faded to yellow, white and green, then flared again to red. The sky had become a kaleidoscope, a glorious, brilliant, ever changing pattern of the most powerful colours.

We gazed up at the display. Only a very small portion of the sky towards the south was dark, the rest of the infinite space above us was a wonderful, awe-inspiring sight. Suitably humbled and reduced in stature we observed the phenomenon until it paled and faded away and the sky became dark once more.

Back to work and, still standing at the foot of the ladder, I looked at Slim.

'I remember that just before the last war the Northern Lights were seen right down in the south of England,' I said. 'It was said that they foretold some awful disaster. Look what happened then, World War Two. Wonder what's going to happen this time?'

Slim was busy fitting slates. 'That's a load of old cobblers,' he said.

'You might well think that,' I replied. 'But time will tell.'

'And we're only wasting time by talking about it.'

Work went ahead again then, but only until we both agreed that we'd had enough for one day. By mid-October the roof was fully slated, we could now work on the inside without any fear that the weather could spoil it.

'Your pup is ready for you.' It was Elsie saying that I could collect my new dog. I couldn't wait and got in the van straight away and went to fetch her. When I walked into Elsie's kitchen the pup came straight to me and we greeted each other like old friends. She had grown quite a bit but although her legs were a little longer she was still plump and her coat was still baby soft.

'What are you going to call her?' asked Edna. Edna was Willie and Elsie's youngest daughter, a pretty girl with big brown eyes.

'I don't know. I hadn't thought about it.'

'I think Floss would be a nice name.'

'I think it would. OK. So Floss it shall be.'

I tucked Floss under my arm and took her out to the van. She sat on the passenger seat as I drove home, sat there and never moved. Although I was sure that she had never been in a vehicle before it was as though to be so was part and parcel of her life already. From that day on, Floss became my shadow.

I had no idea how to train a sheepdog but thought that the first essential should be to sit and stay and to go down the moment the order was given. I worked with her every day, she was quick to learn and eager to please. She padded along behind me all day and seemed to know what I was going to do before I did. If I abruptly turned about she would already be going ahead of me. When I walked out to look at the sheep she cast her eye over them too. By the time she was four months old she showed signs of wanting to work so I thought I would try her.

The first lesson was to pen the flock. When Floss and I walked into the field all the animals calmly walked to the other side, bunched there and turned to look at us. Walking up behind them we quietly herded them round the perimeter fence until they were confronted with the opening of the pen. I stationed myself somewhere between the pen and the tail of the flock and told Floss to send them on. With Floss nipping at their heels and me beating the ground with my crook, in an effort to persuade recalcitrant sheep that it was better to do as they were told, we eventually got them in and the gate closed. We were pleased with our success, Floss waving her tail so madly that the whole of her body swung left and right, and I thinking there was nothing to it after all.

Our next exercise a day or two later was for Floss to round up and bring the flock to me. As we approached them the old ewes gave us no more than a casual glance. I stopped and Floss crouched low beside me, fixed the quarry with her eye and waited for the command. Here goes, I thought, and sent her away, with a yelp of pleasure she was off. She did a good outrun and came up behind them.

'DOWN,' I yelled. 'DOWN.' She took no notice and started to circle the sheep.

'DOWN, DOWN,' I yelled again, but all I got was a contemptuous look as if to say that she wasn't going to let them get away. Again and again I shouted at her, beating the ground with my crook so hard that it was in danger of having loops at both ends. Did she take any notice? Did she hell. Round and round she went until all the old ewes were mesmerised by the constantly circling dog. They stood in a tight knot, chewing the cud, turning their heads to watch her as she passed by.

I gave up and called Floss to me, we would have to do some more homework before I put her to that test again. But first I decided to try to get some advice from an expert. Bertie Tait lived in Ireland, he was a good man with sheep and also at training dogs.

'How can I make Flossie go down when we are out in the field?' I asked him. 'She'll obey me every time when we're at home but when I send her to fetch the sheep she gets them in a bunch and then keeps going round and round.'

'Put her on a long rope,' he said. 'Send her away and command down just before she gets to the end of it. She won't, but the jerk on her neck will give her the lesson she needs.'

I hastened to put his advice into action. I took Floss out into the paddock behind the house. With a long length of rope, actually binder twine off the bales knotted together, attached to her collar, she sat beside me.

'You're going to learn a lesson now Flossie,' I said to her, then gave her the order to, 'Go away'. Off she sped, the pile of twine paying out behind her, as she neared the end of it I shouted, 'DOWN.' But she careered on and the next thing I knew was that I was flying through the air like a nine-pin, my arm almost pulled out of its socket. The jerk on the end of the rope was me. I should have tied the end of it to a fence post or something. Flossie came running back to me, licked my hands as if to say sorry. It was not her fault but the good thing to come out of it was that we had both learned something that day.

We went out daily for our training lessons, for I needed them as much as she. With practice we got our act together and by the time autumn drifted into winter we both knew what we were doing.

With the approach of Christmas once more Slim was again asked to stand in for Santa at the children's party at the Club. Shetland pony and cart were out following last year's performance. The organisers agreed that today's sophisticated children needed a more up-market approach. Santa would descend on the winch rope of a helicopter and be deposited on the balcony of the Clubhouse. Having been on the end of a winch rope many times during his years in the Navy, Slim was more than able to fill the bill.

Dressed in his red suit, false beard and whiskers, sack on his back and

77

winch rope attached he sat in the helicopter waiting for the off. Up they went, flying over the hangars and on towards the Clubhouse. Once again children waited on the balcony and cheered loudly as the helicopter came into view. Positioned over them the pilot held the chopper in the hover for a while. Santa stepped out into the void and was lowered toward the excited children. But he was not to set foot on the balcony this time.

Suddenly the chopper rose in the air, swung away to circle the waters of Sumburgh Voe. Santa, still holding his sack of toys, swung on the end of the rope like a run down yo-yo. Round the voe they went, back across the airfield, made the workers in the control tower smile to see them, before turning again toward the waiting children.

The flight path of the helicopter from the airfield to the Club crossed the road leading to Sumburgh Head. A car was heading that way, radio playing loudly, loud enough to drown the noise of the chopper. Their paths crossed at a vital moment and Santa, complete with sack and in glorious technicolour, sailed through the air before the astonished driver's eyes.

It was rumoured later that he signed the pledge.

Santa landed safely at last, went into the Club and distributed the presents. The children all declared that it was the best Christmas ever.

Christmas came and went. And then on Boxing Day it snowed. Not a lot at first, but then more and more, flakes, big and small drifted down, silently, relentlessly, until everything was covered. The world had assumed a pristine mantle of white, angles had become contours and ugly things a form of beauty.

'It won't last long,' said Slim. 'It never does up here.'

'How can you be sure of that?' I asked.

'Simple, isn't it. There's too much salt in the air. That's the reason ice doesn't stay either.'

'I wouldn't bet on it mate,' I said. 'Remember the Northern Lights? I reckon we've got this for some time. You wait and see.'

But he only laughed at me.

We were back in the daily round, albeit struggling through the snow to go out and feed the sheep. Slim went to work and Michael to school. He had graduated to Sandwick now. He went off just after eight in the morning, down across the fields to the Maywick road where Eenie Smith picked him up in her mini bus to take him to Bigton. From there, with the other children from the Bigton area, he went on the regular bus to the school at Sandwick. He'd not be home until half past four in the afternoon.

I saw him off one morning, a beautiful day, the sky a bonnie blue with never as much as a wisp of cloud in sight, the snow reflecting back the rays of the sun. When Michael had gone then Slim came home, he had been working all night. I gave him some breakfast then left him to go to bed while I did my outside jobs. That done I came in and put the kettle on and, when it boiled, made myself a cup of coffee. Sitting down at the table I picked up the paper that Slim had brought home and started to read it. Engrossed in what I was reading it was some time before I became aware that the wind was getting up. It was making little moaning noises through the cracks round the door. I looked up and out of the window. It was snowing, millions of tiny flakes drifting and dancing before settling. I didn't like it, always thought that small flakes meant business. But it was probably only a shower, it would soon be over. I went back to my paper.

But not for long. Soon the wind round the door was doing more than moan, it cried, then it began to scream and the snow, no longer drifting, came hurtling past the caravan horizontally. It was a blizzard and it didn't look like stopping. It had been ten o'clock when I first realised that it was snowing, it was eleven now. I thought about Michael at school along with all the other children. If the snow drifted and filled the roads, how were they going to get home? I woke Slim and told him what was happening.

'Ring the school if you're worried,' he said. I did.

'Are you going to send the children home?' I asked the head master.

'Their dinner is just about ready, when they've had it we'll let them go.'

'If you don't send them now they won't get home,' I said as I put the phone down.

The blizzard went on for several hours and I knew that no buses were going to travel, how could they? As it neared the time that Michael should have been home the telephone rang. It was the head master from the school.

'Your boy is all right. He is going to stay, with some others, in a house in the village. He'll be home tomorrow.'

Well, I was right. Slim was stuck at home too, but then nothing much was moving for the wind had blown the snow into drifts and it would take some time to clear the roads. Michael came home next day, full of beans at the adventure he'd had. There had been six billeted at the house he was in and boys being boys they had stayed up until midnight playing cards. But then Trevor Burt, whose house it was, came in and read them the riot act and declared lights out.

And the snow? The snow stayed until March and it wasn't until it had nearly all melted away that I went out from Yawfield. After the accident when I'd broken my collarbone I had no wish to venture on icy roads again.

When things eventually returned to normal, or something approaching it, it was time to take stock, to reckon up what we had achieved so far and how much more there was still to do. We had rooted ourselves up from the west of England and put our feet down in this northern land. We had bought a property that needed extensive repairs. We had added twenty-six acres of land to the three that we already had and we now had a flock of sheep. Slim was happy with his work at the airport and Michael was settled at school. School had proved to be a bonus, for instead of the free and easy attitude that prevailed in the schools we'd left behind, the teachers in Shetland were in control and discipline was the order of the day. This year should see the house completed and we'd be able to move in. In April there would be lambs again, lots of them. There was everything to look forward to. It looked as though we were here to stay.

Most of the people I knew went to work, reaping the harvest the oil had brought. Who could blame them, it would not last for ever. Though I spent much time on my own, with just Floss for company, there was plenty for me to do. Along with all the usual housewifely jobs, cooking, cleaning and sewing, I helped where I could with work on the house, looked after the sheep and checked and repaired fences.

Slim left for work at six in the morning and would not be home again before eight at night. Michael was gone at eight and home again eight and a half hours later at four-thirty. No tradesmen called, there was no postman, no milkman, no baker. I picked our letters up at the Post Office in Bigton once a week when I went for my shopping. There was not a soul less than two miles from me. The nearest were an old lady of ninety at Maywick and another younger woman, if she was at home, at Vatster.

One day when I was sitting on the roof of one of the outhouses, trying to repair a hole, I discovered that some of the roof timbers were rotten. If I had fallen through and hurt myself I would have had to lie there for hours before any help came. It gave me food for thought. From then on I decided to check and double check any job I intended to do.

Gardening was something different and something I enjoyed. While working there one day I thought I heard voices. I looked up towards the track expecting to see someone walking along. There was no-one there. I looked down toward the Maywick road, knowing how sound carries in the clear air. I looked up and down the valley but not another human being did I see. Visions of little men sprang to mind. Were they hiding in the grass and watching me? I laughed at my foolishness and thought I shouldn't listen to Willie's tales about the Trows.

But there it was again, the sound of a voice wafting to me on the breeze. My gaze travelled to the road on the other side of the valley and once again I found it empty. I *must* have imagined it. Then a slight movement on the hillside above the road caught my eye. There was someone there. I ran indoors to get the binoculars. I spotted him in the heather, he was lying there with a couple of dogs beside him. Was it a Trow? Well, hardly. Just Gordon Cross taking a day off work and enjoying being with his pets.

I was alone on our hillside most of the time but with Floss for company I was not lonely. I never bothered my head about the Trows any more, not after the last episode anyway. Well... that is until I smelt the smoke. Tobacco smoke it was and what did Willie say? If you smell tobacco smoke you know the Trows are watching you. Even though I got the binoculars out and studied every square inch of the hillsides all around me I never saw another human or found out where the smell of the smoke was coming from.

H. VIGON

CHAPTER ELEVEN

There was no point in having a daily paper because, though sometimes Slim brought one home from work, there never seemed to be enough time to read it. But on Saturdays I made a point of going down to Geordie's at Robins Brae to get one. It was on Saturdays that I visited Willie and Bella Tait. They lived at Ireland and I passed their house on my way home.

I have to confess I had an ulterior motive for calling in. About twelve o'clock on a Saturday morning Bella made bannocks. She used the shining hob on her Rayburn as a griddle on which to cook them. When they were judged to be done on one side she turned them over to finish cooking on the other.

'Would you like a bannock Millie?' asked Bella.

Would I not. 'Yes please,' I said. I knew what I was going to get, a freshly baked bannock, its middle filled with freshly churned butter. The memory of it awakens my taste buds now. While I was sitting in her house, savouring my Saturday treat, a couple of ornaments on the mantelpiece caught my eye. They were creamy in colour, about five to six inches high, four to five in circumference at the base and tapering more or less to a point at the top. They were not rigidly straight but leaned a little, like candles that had got too hot.

I pointed at them and said to Willie, 'What are they?'

'They're whales' teeth,' he said.

'Whales' teeth? Where did you get them?'

'I got them when I was on the whaling ships.'

'Did you go away with the whaling fleet then?'

'Yes.'

'Will you tell me about it? I'd like to know.'

'I could do that.' Willie sat back in his chair and in his soft Shetland accent started to tell me about his time with the whalers.

'When I first went away in 1946 I was just eighteen. It was just after the war and there were very few jobs to be had. I wrote in answer to an advert by Salvesons of Leith; had to write for there were no phones then. They wrote back to say they'd take me but I had to go at once. Another Shetland boy went at the same time.

'We went to South Shields first, there was a factory ship there, the *Southern Venturer*, which had to be got ready for the next whaling season. We were mess boys. We had to wait on twenty-four men in the mess room, fetch the food, wash the dishes and keep the place clean. We were on the *Venturer* for six weeks. From there we went back to Leith to join the S.S. *Saluta*. The *Saluta* was an ex-German supply vessel. We went then to South Georgia, calling at Tenerife on the way for a cargo of fuel oil. The journey took five weeks.'

Geography is not one of my strong points. 'Where exactly is South Georgia, Willie? Isn't it in the Falklands?'

'No, no. It's an island, nothing on it but the whaling stations and a weather station.'

'Must have been a desolate place to go to find work.' I said. 'Wasn't it South Georgia where they found Brunel's iron boat, the S.S. *Great Britain*? Anyway, what did you do when you got there? Did you go out on the boats to hunt the whale?'

'No. I worked ashore. The station was like a big factory. Every trade you could think of was there, machine shop, carpenters, painters, welders. During the winter months the ships were all refitted. We had to scrape, chip and paint in that cold weather. It was hard. The longest time I ever spent there was eighteen months. Just imagine, all that time and only men for company. I think there were four women on the island but they were at the weather station and you were lucky if you happened to catch a glimpse of one of them the whole time you were there. You hear a lot about gays and homosexuality nowadays but all the time I was at South Georgia among hundreds of men it was never apparent. I think people had stricter morals then.'

What a terrible way to make a living, I thought. 'I suppose you worked long hours,' I said. 'Was there any time for recreation and, if so, was there anything to do?'

'We worked a twelve hour day and sometimes overtime as well.' Willie laughed. 'Would you believe we went to the pictures on Saturdays? We used to watch old films. Some of the men used to decorate whales' teeth, you know, draw pictures on them. They did whales' ear drums too. I have a couple, I'll show you.'

He got up from his chair, left the room and came back with something that looked like two carved and painted heads. He turned them round and then they looked similar to large seashells.

'These are the eardrums. They're painted to look like a man and a woman. Here, take a look.'

He handed me one and I was surprised to find it was quite heavy. It was as big as a man's fist.

'I know whales are big, but if this is just an eardrum, how big is a whale?'

'The Blue Whale – and there are not many left – weighs about 90 tons. They reckoned each foot of length equalled one ton.' I was glad he told me that as I wondered how they could weigh a creature that size. 'The biggest I ever saw,' he went on, 'was eighty-eight feet long.'

I tried to imagine an eighty-eight foot long animal. What could I compare it with? Wow. It would have covered the length of a cricket pitch and a bit more besides. Now *that* was a big fish.

'Where were the whales, Willie?' I asked. 'Where were they to be found?'

'They were all over the south Atlantic, mostly the Minke whale round South Georgia. The factory ships went right down to the ice.' For a moment or two he stopped speaking, gazed out of the window, a faraway look in his eye, then he went on. 'The catchers hunted the whale, the first harpoon to be fired had a line attached and the second an explosive charge to kill it. Dead whales were pumped up with air to keep them afloat, ten or so would be tied together and a flag stuck in one of them so that the buoy boats could find them and tow them back, either to the station or to the factory ships.'

'It must have been a rough life, were many men lost?'

'To my knowledge only one catcher was lost, the boat turned turtle and all were drowned except one and that was a Shetland boy called Leask, from Burwick, near Scalloway.'

Nowadays I buy my fish already filleted, I hate having to clean up after when I have to do the job myself, but a herring hardly compares with a whale. How on earth did they tackle that job? I asked Willie how they went about it.

'They were cut up and the blubber boiled in huge cookers to extract the oil. The meat was cooked then dried and made into meat meal. The bones, hauled up to the bone loft, were cut up with a saw that had a twelve-foot blade then thrown down into the cookers. The lids were screwed on and they were steam cooked and processed into bone meal. It was all dried, bagged and stored, then when the cargo boat came in it was loaded on, then ferried home... but it happens no longer.'

He gave a little smile and I asked him if he was glad about that.

'Oh yes. There aren't many whales left. There used to be a lot around Shetland, in fact there were three whaling stations here before the war. I wouldn't like to go back to the whaling. It was a hard life and not good for the women who were left behind, but it was a way of making a living. Men here used to go to the fishing but the rewards were very poor. I remember a time when my father was away for sixteen weeks and when he came home he hadn't made a penny because the fishing was so bad.'

'But did you like being at sea though? I've been told that most Shetland men are good sailors.'

'Well, I was only frightened once and that was when we were caught in a mighty storm in the Roaring Forties. The seas were so mountainous that the old ship trembled and shook like a dog from stem to stern. I thought she was going to fall to pieces and we'd never come out of it... but we did.'

Willie sat at ease in his pleasant house. He would never have to leave his native land again to seek work. The discovery of oil in the North Sea off Shetland had reversed the exodus and brought men and women to it from the four corners of the earth, each one looking for a share of the wealth it promised.

Prosperity ebbed and flowed in and out of the islands like the tide. At least that was the conclusion I had come to from study of some old almanacs that I had found when clearing out our house. With the coming of the North Sea oil boom the tide was in full flood. Carpenters, plumbers, butchers, bakers and many other tradesmen had deserted lowly paid jobs to take advantage of better pay while it was available, even if it was only sweeping a hangar floor or driving a truck at Sullom Voe.

I had seen schoolgirls of about fourteen years of age making deposits of a great deal of money in the banks at Lerwick, money they had earned working as cleaners in the camps where the construction workers from Sullom Voe were housed. They worked in the evenings and at weekends and were transported by bus from Lerwick to the camps. I wondered how long it would be before the tide turned again, how long their savings would last and whether those young people would have to go half way round the world to make a living too.

When I left Willie and Bella that day I was in a very thoughtful mood. The more I got to know the people in whose homeland I had come to live, the more I gained respect for them. Remote and isolated, battered by the wild seas on all sides, living and working in a hostile climate, yet I found them to be kind, generous and hospitable.

I drove slowly up the track towards home, stopping at the top of the hill to open a gate that divided properties. Taking time to stand and stare I looked westward over the peat fields, to the top of the cliffs, beyond which the Atlantic surged and swelled and spread away into infinity. To the south the track snaked down toward Ireland and Bigton with St. Ninians Isle lying just off the coast. Turning to the east I looked across the valley to the far side where the white dots of sheep speckled the hillside. My gaze followed the line of the hill which continued to run northward until it ended somewhere between Scalloway and Lerwick.

I stood there, sheep grazed a few yards from me, quite unconcerned by my presence, seagulls mewed as they floated on the air and the breeze whispered through the hoops of my earrings. In its own way I thought Shetland was a beautiful place... but beauty pays no wages.

Many foreigners have come to the islands, Vikings from Scandinavia, immigrants from Scotland – Shetland had been pledged to Scotland as the wedding dowry of Margaret of Denmark – and who knows who else, and now the foreigners were oilmen and oil-related workers. Slim and I were part of the new wave of incomers.

Slim had travelled the world while serving in the Royal Navy and accepted differing cultures and customs with ease. I had spent the greater part of my life in the counties of Dorset and Somerset and was finding this new way of life to be a constant revelation. We could have lived on one of the estates near the airport, joined in the round of parties and coffee mornings and socialising in general, which was the pattern of life for many of the incomers there, but Slim and I preferred the outdoor life and would have been bored and unhappy any other way.

Before we moved to the croft and had to make hay to feed our animals in the winter, I had watched as the Shetlanders cut their grass, left it to dry, then turn it, pull it into small heaps, then throw them apart again and spread the hay about. Then they stacked it into little heaps again and left it standing for days and weeks before bringing it nearer the barn to be made into a large stack. This they combed with a rake and covered with a net.

Some crofters built a fence with two strands of wire attached and the grass, when it was partly dried, was draped over the wire and again left for many weeks. I thought that the wind and rain would extract all the goodness from it until eventually it would be of little more feeding value than straw, if as good.

There were not many balers in use but the best use was made of those that were, for the crofters tended to work together. Now that we had to make hay for ourselves the reason why Shetlanders made it the way they did was becoming clearer to me.

They say that Shetland has nine months of winter and three of summer. The summer season is definitely short. Grass rarely starts to grow before May and is not ready to cut until July or August. We kissed goodbye the memories of the frantic few days it takes to win a stack of hay in the south and came to terms with the frustrations of hay making in Shetland. We cut our grass, turned it and tossed it to let the wind get through it to dry it. All was going well, but Bobbie Smith warned us that we would have to make it into 'coles', which was what the heaps of hay were called.

'When you have built them,' he said, 'you must comb them so that the hay lies down like a thatched roof, then if it rains most of the water will run off and your hay will be safe. Otherwise the rain will soak in and your hay will be ruined.'

Frustration came when, with spread hay almost dry, the sea mist, laden with salt came whizzing in. It made the hay sticky, it could not be stacked in that condition or it would turn black and rot, so we spread it and tossed it over and over again until I got very fed up with the whole operation. Eventually we got it dried and with great relief were able to stack it in the barn.

Mechanisation of farm work seemed to be a long time getting to Shetland and I often wondered at the old fashioned methods I saw in use. I was amazed one day to see corn being cut with a scythe and a woman tying the sheaves by hand. I couldn't wait to tell Slim when he came home.

'What was the field like where you saw this?' he asked.

'Not very big.'

'And was it on the side of a hill?'

'Yes.'

'There's your answer.'

Talk about smug. Was there ever a question I asked of him that he didn't know the answer to? I was annoyed that I hadn't thought about it myself but many of the fields were small and steep and there was no way I would have driven a tractor on them, so what other way was there to harvest that field of corn? Certainly not by a reaper, tractor and reaper would not have had the room to turn around let alone cut the crop.

The usual method of cutting corn, where conditions permitted, was by binder. The last time I saw one working was during World War Two. A binder cuts the corn, sends it up a canvas conveyer belt, binds the sheaves then throws them out as it travels along. Once it would have been pulled by horses but now the horse power was under the bonnet of a tractor.

The first combine-harvester was brought to Shetland by Jim Budge. Jim lived at Bigton Farm. He was a farmer as opposed to a crofter, working full time on the farm rearing beef cattle and keeping sheep. His family had lived at the farm since 1860. The farm house, an imposing granite building with spacious rooms had once been the residence of the local laird.

At Yawfield we were almost self sufficient in food with the exception of milk and those things we could not grow ourselves. Many people kept a goat to provide milk and after having got used to Nanny we thought it might be a good idea to do the same. Scanning the classifieds in the *Shetland Times* we found one for sale, subsequently bought it and never ran out of milk again.

Goats are very intelligent animals, affectionate and family orientated. They need company and it is not kind to keep just one unless you have lots of time to spend with it. They are browsers and need to roam in order to find the right kind of food for their needs. Keep a goat and you won't need a weather house, with the little man and wife on the wall, for Nanny will tell you when it's going to rain. If she's tethered she'll become agitated and if on free range will seek shelter, she has a thin skin and can become easily chilled. Many times have I rescued my washing from a shower because of my goats.

Our first goat produced two female kids and because she was a good milker herself we decided to keep them. Not only did she provide enough milk for us but for Jimmy and Wendy, our neighbours, too. I don't know if she was fitted with a magnet to attract other goats but they started to arrive at our door from all over the island. One came for a short stay while her owners were on holiday. She had been reared with a pet lamb and was firmly convinced that she belonged to the flock of sheep. She stayed with them, grazed with them and would not come in with the other goats. More goats came from incomers who were leaving the island and didn't know what to do with them. Others were given to me by people who found that caring for a goat was time consuming and also a tie.

Sometimes we'd take our goats for a walk. Crossing the heather to the peat banks the goats would stop and browse here and there then run to catch up with us, dancing along sideways and pretending to fight with each other. There was no fear of them running away for they treated us as leaders of the flock and would follow us anywhere.

From the day I followed Bobbie Mullay's old goat down the road, knowing very little about the animals, my knowledge increased rapidly and it was not long before others were asking my advice. I did not profess to know all there was to know about goats but a little common sense does go a very long way.

My crowning glory came when I was asked to stand in for a friend and judge the goats at the Voe Agricultural Show. A task which I thoroughly enjoyed.

M. Vigors

CHAPTER TWELVE

While I worked outside, tending the sheep, the goats, the garden; while I did the washing, the ironing, the cooking and all the other little jobs women have to do, Slim was beavering away inside the house. As soon as he was finished in a room I got to work with paint and paper and did the decorating. I even built the fireplace in the sitting room, well, it was like building a wall wasn't it, and that's a job I always liked doing. I was a good hand at laying cement too, in fact Slim used to joke and say that he'd married the best bloke McAlpine's ever had.

At long last the job was done and we were ready to move in. Carpets were laid and curtains hung. We took our furniture out of store and put it in the house. At last I was able to open the boxes that contained my books, my ornaments and all sorts of trivia I had packed so long ago. It was with pleasure I removed the wrappings from my pictures and hung them on the wall and a sadness to find a treasured piece of china broken, but it gave me a feeling of contentment to be surrounded with familiar objects once again.

It was nice to have more room to spread ourselves after the confined quarters of the caravan and much more convenient when it came to entertaining visitors. Mimie had come to visit often while we were in the process of renovating the house. Each time she came she marvelled at the changes she saw.

'I thought you were mad when I first saw it,' she said. 'What a lot of work you've done. I couldn't have done it, I couldn't have lived the way you have. You are to be congratulated.'

I suppose that rescuing our house from a ruin could be called a labour of love but Slim had been right when he said it would give him something to do in his time off. I had hardly bargained on it taking up so much of my time though. But it was finished now, we were going to have time on our hands again. Would I have to get another job? I didn't fancy going to work, I was too happy where I was.

'Now that the caravans are empty Slim,' I said, 'what are we going to do with them?'

'You can fill them with chickens.'

'But I don't want any more chickens.'

'You may not but there are a lot of people in Shetland who do. Remember what a lot of trouble you had when you wanted to get some. Find out where to get day old chicks and order three hundred.'

'Are you mad? Where do you think I'm going to sell three hundred?'

'All right then, get a hundred to start with.'

'And what am I going to rear them in?'

'I'll borrow a brooder for you.'

What did I say? He always has the answer. But true to his word the very next day he came home with a brooder box and the paraffin lamp that went with it.

'Where did you get that?' I asked.

'Off Willie Leask. Have you ordered your chicks?'

'Not yet.'

'Well you'd better see to it.'

So I did. The man I spoke to at Muirfield Hatchery in Scotland was very helpful and together we decided that Black Rocks would be the best type of poultry for Shetland's weather. I ordered a hundred day old pullets and when I'd put the phone down set about giving the brooder a good clean. That done, I set it up to make sure it was working properly. It was. When the chicks arrived I'd be in business.

There was no trouble with rail strikes, dockers strikes or gales this time and a day or two later I drove into Lerwick, to collect my chickens. There was great interest when I went to collect them from the P & O transit shed. I was persuaded to lift the lid and was amused to see grown men smiling and cuddling little balls of fluff in large rough hands.

At home the chicks were settled into the brooder, I had lit the lamp before leaving home and checked that it was working well and now the brooder was warm and waiting for them. Within twenty-four hours they were running in and out and feeding quite happily.

Not many days after I had got the chickens Willie and Elsie came to visit and like all good farmers, after we had had a cup of tea and a slice of my best fruit cake, we went out to take a look at the stock. We walked round the sheep, had a look at the calf and the goats and finished up by the chicken house.

'Phoo. What you going to do with all them chickens?' asked Willie.

'I'm going to keep half a dozen for myself and hopefully sell the rest when they're fully feathered and off heat.'

'I'll have a dozen,' he said straight away.

Well, that was an easy sale, I thought, but not as easy as the second. Willie had gone home and about ten minutes after he must have got there he phoned me.

'My uncle over at Rompa will have two dozen of your chicks.'

I couldn't believe it. Slim was right again, there were a lot of people in Shetland who wanted poultry. In the next few days that was borne out time after time, for word got round and the phone was red hot with people wishing to place orders. Any thoughts of saving half a dozen for myself were soon abandoned for I sold the lot and ordered another hundred. This time I managed to save two.

The next year Slim told me to order more, four hundred wouldn't go amiss, he said.

'But I can't keep borrowing Willie Leask's brooder.'

'Advertise for some brooder lamps then and I'll make you some.'

'That's a good idea.'

Shetland Times classifieds came to the rescue again and soon afterwards I acquired the brooder lamps we needed. Slim got to work and in no time at all we had four brooders. We made divisions in the caravans to separate the different lots and then we were ready.

Four lots of chicks need more looking after and often I would get up and go out to them at night to make sure they had enough room and weren't huddling in the corners and suffocating each other. All went well and another advertisement was placed in the paper. Hardly before the printer's ink was dry the phone was ringing and I was taking orders. Twos and threes, sixes and dozens. The orders came from all parts of the islands. From Fair Isle in the south to Unst in the north and from Foula in the west to Skerries in the east.

'Big problem Slim,' I said. 'How am I going to deliver these birds?'

'In your van.'

'But what about the islands?'

'Leave that to me.'

I had no poultry crates so I collected cardboard boxes and orange crates. I cut holes in the sides of the boxes for ventilation, put newspaper and a little hay in the bottom to absorb any droppings. Orange crates were like gold dust but were superior as poultry crates whenever I could get them.

Some of the boxes of chickens were sent by bus. I took some others to the carrier's collection point in Lerwick. Many people living in the outer islands didn't often come into Lerwick but phoned in their orders which were collected and delivered to them by a carrier.

Slim was as good as his word when it came to delivery to outlying islands, either by coercion or by other means he persuaded one of the pilots of the inter-island planes to make delivery.

To send chickens to Fair Isle meant that the box containing the order had to be taken to Grutness pier at Sumburgh and put on the boat, the *Good Shepherd,* and from there across the rough waters of Sumburgh Roost to the island.

I delivered local orders myself. One order for two chickens was for pets for the children. They came out to meet me, took the box from me, carried it into the house where they set it on the floor. Not one word did they say, not even hello. They opened the box and with gentle hands stroked the shining feathers on the backs of the chicken. I had expected the birds to fly out in fright, but no, they seemed to like the treatment they were being given. Then the children picked the chickens out from the box and holding them in their arms, smiled at me. Still not a word did they say, I am sure they were not dumb, probably just shy. Their mother thanked me and paid me and I came away thinking that children were the strangest things.

I was welcomed wherever I went and at every house I was offered tea and biscuits or cake. At times I had difficulty understanding the dialect and at others it was no problem. Strangely enough at one place where the husband and wife were both deaf and dumb I had no trouble at all in understanding or being understood. Not so when I met the younger generation.

Michael and I took a box of chickens to a house at Gulberwick. It was built on the side of the hill and was sort of upside down, for the bedrooms were downstairs and the kitchen and living room on the upper floor. I went to the door and knocked. There was no reply. I knocked again and again but still no one came. There were children playing in the garden which was below me. A boy of about ten and some younger ones who looked to be under five.

'Is your mother at home?' I asked the older boy.

'Yes. She's inside. Go in.'

I wasn't used to walking in to a stranger's house, it wasn't done where I came from, but I opened the door and called, 'Hello.' There was no reply so I pushed open the door and went in, through the kitchen and into the living room. The place was empty and I felt like an intruder so I beat a hasty retreat. Outside on the step again I looked down into the garden. The eldest boy had gone and only a little one was there.

'Is your mother at home?' I asked him.

He looked up at me with puzzlement on his face. 'Eh?' he said. I repeated the question only to be met with the same puzzled, 'Eh?'

'He doesn't understand me,' I said to Michael and then proceeded to do what all English people do when in foreign parts. I spoke slowly and clearly.

'Is... your... mother... at.... home?'

He was really confused now. 'Eh?' he said.

'He doesn't understand English, Mike.'

'Well, speak Shetland then.'

I leaned over the railings, looked down at the child below me, this was going to have to be my last attempt.

'Is de midder hame?'

A look of joy lit up the little face. 'Ay. Inside.'

At that moment the house door opened and mother appeared. Our troubles were over.

Two orders arrived for customers on the north isles, one on Yell and one on Unst. Here was an excuse for a day off and a chance to see what the northern isles looked like. There were other boxes of chickens to be loaded for the collection point in Lerwick, I put them all in the van, locked the door and set off.

It was a fine day for a change. There was not a lot of sunshine but the air was fresh and keen. I left the boxes of chickens for the carrier and decided that while I was in Lerwick I had time to buy the few groceries that I required. That done I turned the van towards the north and began to travel a new road.

Driving north from Lerwick I was surprised to find that the road was much wider and obviously newer than those in the south of the island. It was clear that it had recently been constructed and I concluded that it had been built to accommodate traffic to and from Sullom Voe during the construction of the oil terminal there. In places the old road was still visible and it was obvious that it had been totally unsuitable for the huge lorries rumbling back and forth.

I drove through a barren landscape, skirted a long valley that appeared brown and stagnant. Peaty mounds topped with rushes were interspersed with pools of water. A few scraggy sheep grazed there. I passed lochs of still water with better land beside them. Deserted croft houses littered the area. When I looked at them and the barren infertile land surrounding them I wondered how anyone could ever have made a living from it. Here and there were a cluster of occupied houses, the fences good and the gardens neat.

The village of Voe was a surprise. Pretty and green, it looked like a good place to live. Voe is the name for a long sea inlet. The village had been built round the head of the voe, the waters of which were flanked on either side by the steeply rounded contours of the hills. Though I gave it only a glance as I drove through, it was enough to make me promise myself that I would pay it a proper visit at some later date.

Leaving the village behind me, my route passed through a sheltered valley where cattle grazed. The road began to climb the side of a hill. Carved out of the hill side the incline was steady and the road straight, as it climbed higher the view grew wider. Across a narrow strip of water a hill rose steeply, too steep even for sheep to graze. Below me a finger of land, on which a house stood, protruded into the water. What an odd place to build. When the sea raged, as it often did, the water must surely come in at the front door. But then maybe it wasn't a dwelling house, but a haaf station. Small islands, some little more than rocks dotted the waters here.

When the weather is calm and the sky not a grey, heaving mass, the sea takes on a blueness that would not be out of place in the Med. This was such a day. There were not many travellers on the road so I dawdled, taking time to absorb the newness of my surroundings. Reaching the crest of the hill at last the road turned away from the sea and carried me past the village of Firth. There was a camp there to house the workers who were building the terminal at Sullom Voe. From Firth I then followed the road for Toft, where I was to get the ferry for Yell.

At Toft there was also a camp, in fact the camps were self contained villages with bars, snack bars, cinema and sports complex.

I had not long to wait for the ferry and was soon on board. I got out of the van and leaned over the ship's rail to look into the water. The colour of it changed constantly, pieces of wood drifted by, bouncing and tossing as the bow wave of the ship pushed them out of the way. I searched all the time for porpoises and longed to see a whale but I saw nothing more than small fish moving.

Yell consists of ninety per cent peat I'd been told. I had to cross Yell to get to the ferry for Unst but the only way to cross it was to go round it for that was the way the road went. Croft houses bordered the road and the land about them was green and looked good. The green land of Yell was a narrow strip, separated from the hill of brown peat by the road.

After some time the road turned east then north and by a convoluted route reached Gutcher. As I drove down the road towards the pier I was devastated to see the ramp being hauled up. As I stopped the van by the water's edge the ferry was pulling away. I had missed it literally by the skin of my teeth. Never mind, I thought, it will be back again in half an hour.

I got out and walked about a bit to stretch my legs. I looked about me but there was nothing much to see. A pile of stones where there had once been a building, a couple of sheep, a few sea birds and the sea slapping lazily on the rocks. It was very peaceful.

I looked towards the place where the ferry had berthed, watched for signs that it was preparing to come back. But nothing moved. A glance at my watch told me it was one o'clock, must be lunchtime. I would have to wait another half hour for I didn't think they would be back before two o'clock. What a nuisance.

I had not thought to bring sandwiches or coffee with me and the pangs of hunger were beginning to pinch my stomach. Ah, but there was a box of groceries in the van though, biscuits, yoghurt, bananas and a pint of milk were in my basket along with other things. I munched my way through the biscuits, but they made my mouth dry so I drank the milk.

To pass the time I tried to doze but could not. I looked constantly at my watch alternately studying the harbour across the sound for any sign that the ferry was returning. Two o'clock came and went and still there was no sign of movement on the other side. I wondered if the ferry men had gone on strike.

With nothing else to eat I started to unzip the bananas. When they were gone the yoghurt was next on the list. I would have given my eye teeth for a cup of tea just then.

After what seemed to be an eternity I saw the ferry at last nosing its way toward me. It was a great relief to get on board at last and know that I was on the last leg of my journey.

Unst, as much as I saw of it, was lush and green in comparison to Yell. Following the directions that had been given me I was soon driving into a yard before a croft house. Dogs came running and barking with their lady owner following close behind. She welcomed me and I went to get her chickens from the van.

'No. Leave them,' she said. 'You must be wanting a cup of tea.'

Magic words. I fervently agreed and followed her into the house. She invited me to sit at the table. In front of me was a knife, fork and spoon. I didn't need them to drink tea. And then she was carrying in a bowl of broth, setting it down before me.

'You must be hungry,' she said.

Hungry? My stomach was full of my groceries. Where was I going to find room for the soup? Not wishing to offend her by refusing I plodded my way through it. Thankful at last to put my spoon down I was dumbfounded when she whipped away the empty dish and replaced it with a plate containing a meat pie, vegetables and gravy. Again I struggled, loosened my belt and carried on. Then, and only then, tea was poured and a plate with a gorgeous sponge cake put on the table. The tea was welcome but the sponge was too much. If I had known all this was waiting for me I would have gladly starved half to death on Gutcher pier.

It was not until after I had been fed and watered and she had plied me with many questions that my customer decided it was time to take delivery of her chickens. We took them to the house that was to be their home and when they had been safely installed I was allowed to leave.

The welcome this crofter's wife had given me was typical of the Shetland people I had met so far. They were genuine in their welcome to the stranger at their door.

The journey home never seems as far as that away from it. I didn't miss either of the ferries on the way home and was soon driving in and out of Lerwick and along the bumpy, twisting road to the south.

Rearing chickens seemed to be a success. Slim helped me in any way he could, but in the caravan one day, with little chickens darting about all over the place, I told him to be careful where he put his feet. So what did he do? He promptly stepped on one and broke its leg.

'Have to wring its neck now,' I said.

'No we won't.'

'Can't sell a chicken with a broken leg.'

'We'll put a splint on.'

'Oh yea,' I said. 'With what?'

Why is it that sailors are so damned good at getting out of a sticky situation? After rooting round in my kitchen Slim came up with a couple of iced lolly sticks and some black sticky tape. Deputising me to hold the chicken, he wrapped the sticky tape round them.

'There you are,' he said. 'Good as new. Well, it will be.'

'We shall have to make sure we take that splint off before we sell it, can't sell a chicken with a wooden leg.'

But we did forget didn't we and I think it went with an order of a couple of hundred.

Rearing chickens and delivering them to people gave me the chance to learn more about their way of life. It gave me other chances too, like the chance to add to my animals. The calf I had got from Andrew was doing well and I hoped that I would be able to get another some time. I didn't know how soon that was going to be.

Off once more on my round of deliveries I took a box of chickens to Mr Halcrow at Cunningsburgh. He was a farmer and of course, the talk, as it always does, turned to farming. He asked me how I liked living up at Yawfield and how we were getting on. I told him how we had rescued the house, how I had goats as well as sheep and one stot calf.

'I'd like to get some more,' I said.

'Come and have a look in here then,' he said and opened the door to a cow stall. 'I got someone to buy a cow for me in Aberdeen market and she calved in the market place, that's the calf there.'

In the corner on a bed of straw lay a little black and white calf.

'What is it, male or female?'

'It's a heifer.'

'Would you sell it to me?'

'I would.'

'Oh, brilliant.'

I'd only had to take one look at that calf to fall in love with it. I asked Mr Halcrow how much he wanted for it, agreed to what he said, shook hands and said I'd come and fetch it on my way home. I didn't stop to drink too many cups of tea that day.

At home I put the calf in the end of the barn and from then on waited impatiently for Slim to come home so that I could show him what I'd got. He was as delighted as I when he saw the little thing.

'What are you going to call her?'

'Hadn't thought about that.'

'Well I think she's a little Lulu.'

'Lulu. That's a nice name. We'll call her Lulu.'

'Did you get any calf milk for her when you were in town?'

'I did.'

'And what about a teat.'

'Don't want one of those, she'll drink out of a bucket. Well, she will when I've taught her.'

And she did, and she thrived, and the other calf was pleased to have another for company instead of the independent goats.

We were settling in now in more ways than one. In some ways coming to Shetland had been like taking a step back in time. The pace of life was slower, community spirit stronger. Entertainment still centred on the village hall and not on what was spilling out of a TV set. It was safe to leave a car unlocked, also the doors of the house. In many homes there was still room for the old folk. Crime was negligible. Some drunkenness, some fights, an occasional arrest for driving too fast in a built up area and some petty thieving but nothing more serious.

How soon would the persuasive voice of advertisements on the television screen and glimpses of what appears to be a life of comfort with all mod cons, two cars in the garage and foreign holidays, begin to sow the seeds of discontent in the young?

Youth looks forward but age looks back. Was that what we were doing? Trying to recreate the atmosphere of our childhood? If so, in Shetland, we had found the right place to do it.

CHAPTER THIRTEEN

From my kitchen window I looked south, through the valley, towards Vatster, on to where the Bigton Church stood, quite divorced from the village, and on again to Mossy Hill and the early warning dishes on top of it. In the bottom of the valley lay Vatster loch, half a mile of water from which I took my readings as to the state of the weather. I could tell which way the wind was blowing and from the motion of the water's surface, be it ripples or waves, tell how strong it was.

Michael liked to fish and spent many an hour casting his line from the side of the loch. At our end of it lay the carcase of a boat, it had belonged to Bobbie Smith but had long since been abandoned and was quietly rotting away. Michael examined it closely and wondered if it could be made good again.

'No chance,' said his father.

'What I'd really like,' said Michael, 'is a boat. I'd stand a better chance of getting something if I could get out in the middle of the loch. I get nothing from the side.'

But boats were not that easy to come by so he continued to stand and fish at the water's edge, though his eyes often strayed to the middle where the fish were jumping.

'Hi Mike. I think I've found you a boat.'

Michael's eyes lit up as though all his Christmases had been rolled into one. 'Oh great. What's it like?'

'It's a marine ply rowing boat with a flat bottom. It's going cheap.'

'How much?'

'A crate of beer will make it yours.'

'Brill. Thanks Dad.'

When the boat came home and I saw it for the first time I thought it wasn't much to look at. It needed it's seams caulked and a lick of paint before it could go in the water. But this was no deterrent for Mike. All other forms of entertainment were put aside for the tar pot and the paint brush. The only pot of paint that was available was blue, so blue it had to be. When the work had been done and she was declared to be seaworthy all that was left to do was to give her a name.

Suggestions were made and abandoned. *Blue Lady* was put forward because she had been painted blue, but a lady she was not. We racked our brains for something suitable but could think of nothing appropriate. Then someone said that as she was flat, top and bottom, she should be called *The Dab*, so *Dab* she became and in rather shaky letters Michael wrote her name on her bows.

'Now that you've got your boat she ought to be properly launched. We should get someone to come and christen her,' I said.

The idea was thought to be a good one so I asked a friend if she would do the honours.

'But remember Freda,' I told her, 'you must wear the regulation picture hat, use the time honoured words, I name this ship etcetera, etcetera, and speak with a very posh accent.'

Freda promised to do just that.

On the day of the official launch the *Dab* was already in the water, her nose pushed into the bank. A celebration tea had been prepared, was waiting indoors and all we needed now were the principal players.

Freda, accompanied by her husband and her children, arrived on time. As promised she was wearing a picture hat, bright yellow it was and certainly floppy brimmed. Pity it was a sou-wester, but still, it was apt. She carried her youngest child in a sling on her back. The other was sensibly clad in a waterproof suit. Other friends joined us and we all trooped down to where the *Dab* rode the water.

Freda stepped forward and recited in a too, too refined voice, 'I name this ship *The Dab*. May God bless her and all who sail in her.'

Now, we'd replaced the bottle of bubbly with a can of beer, couldn't spread broken glass around, it wasn't good for animals feet. Giving the can a good shake Freda leaned forward, pulled the ring tab and sprayed *Dab's* bows with beer. When she straightened up again I was relieved to see that the baby was still on her back, I had been afraid that she might fly over her mother's head and receive an unexpected baptism in the loch.

As we had no slipway, a volunteer was pulling on a rope attached to the *Dab* that stretched across the loch and so the little boat rode gently across the water. We cheered and clapped our hands.

It was my turn now to step forward and present our celebrity with a bouquet. Cultivated flowers did not grow in my garden so the content of it was entirely original, buttercups, clover and anything else I could find all tastefully wrapped in a rhubarb leaf and tied with binder twine. I curtsied, not a very elegant one I confess, well it's not easy when you're wearing an anorak and Wellington boots, and gave her the flowers. She thanked me, then, practical soul that she was, upended the beer can and drank the rest of its contents. We repaired to the house, to the celebration tea and for the next hour or two enjoyed the company of our friends.

The launch had been a success. The boat was an even bigger one. It was frequently on the loch and a happy boy caught many a fresh trout for us.

The road to our house was in a bad state of repair. Until we came to live at Yawfield it had only been used by people going to the peat fields and by others who had stock in that area, and for that purpose it was adequate. The occupants of the other two houses in our township didn't use the track but preferred to leave their cars on the other side of the valley and walk home across the fields.

Even though the track was full of potholes, Slim and I preferred to drive home. We attacked it in different ways. I drove carefully, skirted the biggest holes and drove slowly to avoid damaging the suspension of my vehicle. Slim drove at speed, saying that the momentum of the van prevented him from dropping into the holes. Nevertheless, the holes got deeper and the puddles wider. I talked to Willie Tait about it and he told me that once a year the council gave out free road stone for the repair of tracks such as ours. A notice would be put in the paper and anyone requiring stone should apply.

When the notice appeared I applied for road stone for the occupants of the other two houses as well as for ourselves. We were granted six, sixteen-ton lorry loads of scalpings, they were delivered and off loaded at various points along the track. We had enough to fill an awful lot of holes. Two of the loads were tipped at the Ireland end of the track. There was a gate across it there and Bertie Tait's gathering pen for his sheep beside it.

It was Friday evening when Bertie phoned to tell us that a lorry would be coming to pick up some of his sheep on the following Monday.

'The only place the lorry can turn,' he said, 'is where the stone has been tipped. Do you think you could move it?'

I said I'd see what I could do. Thirty-two tons of stone, it would need more than a wheelbarrow and shovel to shift that lot.

'Bertie Tait wants us to move all that stone down by the Ireland gate, Slim,' I said. 'I don't know how we're going to do that, do you?'

'Why does he want it shifted?'

'Because a lorry is coming to pick up his sheep on Monday and the stone is in the way.'

'That's a bit of a bind isn't it,' said Slim. 'But we aren't the only people to use the track, why don't you ask that lot in Ireland if they can't come and help. They all use it to go to the peat and their stock.'

'How right you are.'

I fetched the phone book and started to dial numbers.

'Hello Willie. Bertie's asked me if we'll move all that stone by the Ireland gate as the lorry is coming for his sheep on Monday. We've only got a wheelbarrow, I wonder if you could give us a hand tomorrow?'

'Ah, well, I dunna ken what I'm doing tomorrow.' My heart sank, here was a refusal I was sure. 'But I'll come if I can.'

Well that was a yes and a no in one. I dialled the next number and the conversation I had then was, as near as dammit, identical, word for word. And at every other number I called it was the same thing. They didn't think they would be able to but they'd come if they could.

Saturday dawned. I made a flask of coffee and put some biscuits in the bag beside it while Slim and Michael were putting the wheelbarrow, some shovels and a rake into the van. With grave misgiving about what the day was going to bring we climbed in and set off down the track. When we got to the gate the thought of moving all that stone with the equipment we'd got was like emptying a swimming pool with a sand castle bucket. There was no sign of any activity in the village so we parked the van by the fence and decided to have a cup of coffee before we started. We sat in the van and looked at the houses in Ireland. Nothing moved.

We heard the sound of the tractor first, it was starting up and we wished it was ours. We could do with it. And then it came in sight. It was coming our way, but there was a fork in the road, it could be going to Claypots. It was Robert Morrison and his little old Fergie and it was pulling a trailer. Our eyes were glued to him and we were all willing him to bear left and come on up to us. He did and we began to smile.

Another figure appeared. It was Willie Tait. Two pairs of helping hands, this was great, but there was more to come. Willie Leask came, also with a trailer, closely followed by Johnnie Morrison with his sons, Brian and Nigel. This was getting better and better. Michael's school friend Maurice came next, on a big tractor with a digger bucket on the front.

We had a road gang. Our smiles turned to broad grins.

The men went into a huddle then, worked out a plan of action and promptly set about it. Soon the piles of stone rapidly diminished until the two by the gate were completely gone. No need to stop now, they said, and proceeded to distribute the next two lorry loads. The trailers were in constant action, Robert Morrison's was rather ancient, the tipping action had to be done by hand by winding up a screw, but it worked and was still in good nick, there was no point in getting another. Those of us without mechanical means of distributing stone, raked at it in an effort to get it reasonably level. We all worked until lunchtime and between us moved about eighty tons of stone.

It had been a heart-warming experience to see our friends and neighbours give up their time to help us and another confirmation that the community spirit in Shetland was very much alive. We thanked them with all our hearts, watched as they drove off down the now repaired track, then loading our wheelbarrow, an item unused, in our van along with the shovels, we turned and made for home.

As autumn approached the lambs would have to be separated from their mothers. With Flossie's help I gathered the flock in the pen, picked up the lambs and dropped them outside. Now we would drive them into another field. They bunched together and meekly went before us in the right direction. When they reached the open gate into the next field they hesitated, refused to be driven through and split away in all directions. Back across the field we went, Floss and I, to gather them once more. Again they would not pass through the gate. Time after time we got them to it but not through it. But I was not about to give up and we gathered them again, drove them down the field to the gate. With tempers now on very short fuses we seemed to have won at last when finally one after another they trotted through. All but the last one. As I was about to swing the gate shut behind him he turned on a sixpence and sprinted away.

It was the last straw. With a roar of rage I was after it as fast as my legs would go. Floss lost her temper too, but she was quicker than I. Together dog and lamb raced across the field, with a flurry of legs they tangled, somersaulted, were up and off again. I ran in pursuit. We all ran, the dog, the lamb and I, 'til my legs ached and my throat burned as I gasped for breath.

Finally all three of us came to a halt beside the gathering pen. With my heart beating a tattoo in my chest I fell to the ground with exhaustion. Floss collapsed beside me, red tongue lolling, mouth a wry grin as she sucked in her breath. All thought of flight gone, the lamb stood on my other side, his flanks heaving as he too gulped air. He was so close that if I reached out my hand I could touch him.

Presently I became aware of the soft bleating of lambs and the answering voices of the ewes. All the lambs had come back. No use trying to separate them again that day so, letting the ewes out of the pen I watched as ewes and lambs gambolled across the park, mother matching up with child as they went.

Autumn is the time of the sheep sales. All animals surplus to requirements are sold. Lambs that were born in the spring are inspected and the best ewe lambs kept for breeding the following year. The remainder, as well as old ewes and rams whose useful life is over are sent to the market.

There are three ways to sell sheep in Shetland. One way is farm to farm sales. The auctioneers and buyers travel from farm to farm, or croft, where the sheep that are to be sold are penned in a yard or by the roadside. The second way is to transport them to the market place in Lerwick, the third to transport them again to Lerwick, put them on the boat and send them to the market in Aberdeen.

As our croft was at the end of a rough track Bobbie Mullay said I could use his pen on the other side of the valley and as his land joined ours I was grateful for the offer. I herded the lambs I had for sale across the little bridge over the stream and then up and into the pen. The auctioneers and buyers would be on their way so I sat by the roadside to wait. I had decided how much the lambs were worth and made up my mind that I wasn't going to let them go for a penny less.

At last a cavalcade of cars approached. They parked in a line by the side of the road and a dozen or so men got out. I'd seen men like that before. They wore tweed trousers, jumpers and body warmers and on their feet were dealer's boots, boots of tan leather, thin leather, decorated with punch work. I never trusted men who wore dealer's boots.

The auctioneer made himself known to me, asked if the sheep were mine and if they were for sale. Then he started the auction. The bidding was desultory and did not reach the sum I had decided on so I intervened and said I wouldn't sell them at that price. Shock and surprise were written all over the faces that were turned to me. The auctioneer took me by the arm and led me a few paces away. He asked me what sum I wanted and when I told him, said it was too much.

'Well, I shan't sell them then,' I said. 'I know what they're worth.'

And I didn't sell them. I watched the buyers as they got in their cars and drove away. When I saw Bobbie Mullay a day or two later he asked me why I hadn't sold my lambs.

'Robbin' bastards,' I said. 'They must have thought because I'm a woman they could put one over on me.'

'Where are you going to sell them now?' he said.

'Market?'

'If you take them to the market you'll see the same buyers and it will cost you money to get them there.'

'All right, Aberdeen then.'

'Same buyers there, they come up here for the sales you see. It'll cost you even more to get them to Aberdeen, you have to get them to Lerwick and it'll cost you at least £5 a head to put them on the boat. The buyers in Scotland will know you won't be able to take them home so you'll be forced to take what they offer.'

It was a catch 22 situation, Hobson's choice, take it or leave it. Once more the cost of freight to and from the islands was the culprit. The more I thought about it the angrier I got. Why should people living on an island be penalised in this way? It wouldn't happen on the mainland. I got even angrier realising there was nothing to be done about it.

I was going to have to sell my lambs somewhere, there wasn't room enough to keep them all. The ewe lambs were good, they were Cheviot crosses, I advertised them in the paper and they all sold at a good price. Admitting defeat I sent the hogs to Aberdeen where, after deductions they paid me even less than I had been offered at the road side. That was a lesson hard learned, but weighing it all up, and combining all the money I had got, I hadn't done too bad.

We had bought ourselves a tractor, a little old grey Fergie to which had been added a front loader. It would ease the load of many jobs around the croft, such as taking out the manure from the byres where the calves lived. We had four calves now, I had bought two more Hereford cross heifers from Mr Halcrow. It would also be useful for picking up stone when we had a day at road mending. We could not always expect the residents of Ireland to be willing to help us whenever we asked them. The Fergie was a real bargain, Slim had a nose for them. One day when he came home he told me he had bought a dumper.

'What on earth did you want to do that for?'

'I thought Michael would like it.'

I smelled a rat. 'Funny present for a boy,' I said.

'Ah, but I have an ulterior motive.' I might have known.

'Now why doesn't that surprise me. What is it?'

'He can use it to shift the road stone for the track.'

'But we've already got a tractor and loader.'

'That's right. Now he can use it to load the dumper. You didn't think that he'd load the dumper by hand did you?'

No, I didn't. Most of today's youth is averse to working with hand tools and Michael was no exception to the rule. When he got home from school and saw the dumper sitting there he was delighted and couldn't wait to use it.

All Shetland boys whose fathers had crofts became very competent drivers at an early age. Michael drove the tractor and Brian Jamieson, his friend from Ireland, the dumper. Together they worked at repairing the road. No matter what the weather, rain or shine, most weekends saw them hard at it.

Wet weather came in varying degrees of severity. Sometimes rain lashed down, sometimes just fell and sometimes swirled about and was just a little wetter than mist. It had been a day like this in November and Michael and Brian had been out since early morning. It was cold as well as wet so I thought I would take them a warming flask of coffee and some cake.

To protect myself from the cold I put two woolly jumpers on top of a vest and shirt, long johns under my trews, and two pairs of socks. I topped it all off with the regulation blue anorak, crammed a woolly hat on my head and pulled on my wellies. I was now as wide as I was high but I didn't care, at least I was warm.

Picking up the bag with the goodies I set off to walk to where the boys were working. When I reached them they were in a very happy mood, wide grins creased their faces and laughter bubbled up as they spoke. When I asked what it was that was making them so cheerful all they would say was, 'Nothing, nothing.' It was not true of course but they would say no more.

I met Brian's father a day or two later and said to him how well I thought the boys were doing. I told him I'd taken them some coffee and that I'd been down to see how they were getting on.

'Yea,' he said. 'Brian told us you'd been down. He said he'd seen this peerie wife coming down the track, muffled up with dozens of coats and he "tot it was a peerie Trow".'

He laughed and so did I. I'd never been mistaken for a Trow before.

CHAPTER FOURTEEN

As the year draws to a close the cycle of the next crofting year begins. Our flock of ewes had been sorted out, the oldest ones culled and a half dozen gimmers, eighteen-month-old ewe lambs brought in. I had bought a Cheviot ram and he had been introduced to his wives in December, with luck they would all lamb the next April. All the surplus lambs that had been born in the spring were now off the croft. We had made and stored enough hay for the winter and bought in concentrates for the ewes' winter feed. Although it was unlikely that we would get another winter of snow and ice we thought it wise to be prepared.

Our own larder was well stocked. The freezer was full of homebred lamb and surplus vegetables from the garden. There was also milk there too, for goats' milk freezes well and does not deteriorate when thawed out. In a corner of the cupboard in the kitchen was a bottle or two of whisky, some of our friends were partial to a dram and it would be unthinkable not to have some to offer them should they come calling.

Christmas Day passed quietly and Boxing Day started that way too, but just as we had settled down to spend a quiet evening we heard the sound of a motor coming to a stop outside. Car doors slammed, there was a knock on the door but before we could get to it to open it, Willie Leask walked in and right behind him came his neighbour, Johnnie.

'We thought it was time we paid you a visit,' said Willie while Johnnie nodded assent.

'We're very glad you have, take a seat. You'll have a dram, won't you?'

Did I really need to ask? I fetched the bottle and some glasses and liberally splashed the bottoms of them. In no time at all we were laughing at the tales Willie had to tell.

'There was a man who decided to kill his bullock,' he said. 'It was a good one. He did the deed in an outhouse then tried to haul it up to a rafter. But the rafters were rotten and as the bullock went up the roof came down. Ha ha ha.' Visions of the bullock and its owner sitting in a pile of tiles and rotten timbers made us all laugh. 'It didn't hurt the bullock,' Willie went on, 'because it was already dead and the crofter didn't come to much harm, just a few cuts and bruises. The carcase was bigger than he thought though, and he and his family were fed on mince and tatties for months afterwards. He ended up giving half of it away.'

Sheep were easier to cope with, he said. 'But Shetlanders never eat offal, it filters all the muck. And we don't eat mushrooms either, think about what they grow in.'

'You know Millie, my father bought this place, the house we're in now, in nineteen-thirtyeight, for the grand sum of one hundred pounds.' Willie had grown up at Yawfield. 'For that he got a house, a byre for seven cattle plus calves, and two or three outhouses. The land itself was held under crofting tenure for which rent was paid. The freehold was finally purchased twenty-six years later.

We had twenty-five acres of windy hillside, five of them were said to be arable, plus a share of the outrun. We did plough some of the land with a pony and a very light plough.'

Willie went on to tell us of the skills he had learned as a boy, cutting divots or flaas, a thin turf for covering the roof of the house. Cutting peat, milking the cow, working with the horse and all the hundred and one jobs that have to be done on a croft. He was also skilled at curing and dressing sheep skins.

'When I look at the land today,' he said, 'I think my father must have been very optimistic even to think we could exist in such a place. When we were moving in one of the neighbours asked if he was right in the head. There was no road to the house when we came here and the ground was too steep for a horse and cart so our furniture was hauled in by a neighbour with a horse and sledge. In fact all the neighbours came to help, it was a break in the usual routine you see. We were the last people to move into the valley until you people came, after my family moved in all the moves were out.'

It was very interesting to hear some of the history of Yawfield. Willie told us about the people who lived in the other houses and how one by one they died or moved away. I had often wondered how anyone could make a living on such poor land, we were lucky in that Slim was the bread winner and we did not have to rely on the croft to make us a living. I had grown up with farming and was well aware of its drawbacks.

But there was something else I wanted to know. From our top fields we could see the island of South Havera and the ruins of several houses there. The island was no longer occupied but it looked attractive and I had looked at it and longed to go there.

'Is there any way of getting over to Havera?' I asked.

'Havera? You want to go there? Robbie Adam would take you in his boat if you ask him.'

'What can you tell me about the place?'

'Well, there were five houses occupied at one time and they had a school teacher for all the children. There were two cows kept to provide milk for them all. When the cow had to be mated they put her in the boat to bring her across to the mainland, but the bottom of the boat had a rotten timber and the cow's foot went through. One of the old fellers rolled up his jacket and stuffed it in the hole. They had a halter on the cow so they off loaded it and made it swim behind the boat.'

'Oh yes, pull the other one.'

'No, that's true,' said Johnnie.

'I don't believe you.' But I laughed all the same.

'Another time,' said Willie, 'they brought the cow over and, because the men were busy at something else, left one of the young women to take the cow on to the bull. The man who owned the bull was young and handsome and when the cow and the girl went back to the island they were both pregnant.'

There were shouts of laughter at this and I noticed that the whisky glasses were dry. 'Have another drink,' I said and fetched the whisky bottle.

So far Willie had done all the talking, Johnnie had just sat back in his chair listening and laughing at what Willie was saying. But now he spoke.

'I did hear that one time, when all the men on Havera were away fishing and the women had taken the boat to Scalloway to sell their knitting and taken the kids with them, there was only one old couple left on the island.'

Johnnie's face was quite serious but I just happened to glance at Willie and saw the ghost of a smile starting to cross his face. I wondered what was coming next.

'While the women were in Scalloway,' said Johnnie, 'a storm blew up and they couldn't get back. On the island the old man died. Well that was bad enough but the storm went on for days and the old lady was in a bit of a fix. She couldn't get any help, for the boat was gone, and she couldn't have rowed it anyway. She had to do something with the old man, but she wasn't strong enough to dig his grave so she did the only other thing she could do... she salted him down like a leg o' mutton.'

Then Johnnie laughed. Slim was rolling around in his chair, Willie spluttering over his whisky and I was laughing 'til my sides ached. From then on the tall tales came thick and fast and as always when in good company the time just flew away. Midnight came and went and we were in to the small hours. Reluctantly we had to say, not goodnight to our visitors but good morning, wish them a safe journey and hope they would return again soon.

Even though sleep that night was but an hour or two there was no chance to lie in, our livestock were dependent on us to feed them so we had to rise.

Now that they had grown in number we needed to grow more food for them. The kale yard was not big enough so we thought it would be a good idea to plough up some more land. Just below the house there was a flat area which looked as though it had been ploughed before. We had bought a hill plough and Michael was willing to be ploughman. He had never ploughed before so he asked his friend Maurice for advice. Not only did Maurice come to show him how to plough, he also stayed to help and together they did a good job. Some huge stones were uncovered which had to be pulled out of the ground by the tractor, but the earth looked good when the job was done. When the boys had finished I set to work with the cultivator to render the furrows down to a tilth fit for seeds to be sown in.

To mark out the rows I made a tool which I had first seen in Cornwall. It was like a giant rake, but with only four teeth. A piece of wood about four foot six inches long, or thereabouts, was fitted with four teeth about eighteen inches apart. A handle was then attached with two bracing struts. In Cornwall it was used to square off a field for setting violet plants. They flower all winter, I grew them there, picked them and sent them to Covent Garden flower market.

I was going to have to sow my seeds with the aid of a tool designed for use in a garden and would first have to mark out the rows. To do this I dragged the rake across the field in as straight a line as I could, then, turning around and setting the end tooth in the last furrow the process was repeated, thus marking three more rows. When I'd covered the whole plot I was ready to put in the seed. The variety of swede called Marion was put in, the rows tamped down then left for nature to take her course, aided and abetted by the woman with the hoe.

In April it was announced that the Queen would be coming to Shetland to declare the oil terminal at Sullom Voe officially open. She would leave the islands by plane from Sumburgh airport. Children were to have a day off school and though I thought it would be silly to miss a chance to see her, I didn't fancy being jostled in the crowd of people I was certain would be there. Not only that, being only five foot tall, not being on the front line meant I might just as well not be there at all. All I ever see if I'm stuck in a crowd is the back of somebody's neck. Better to stand at the side of the road if only to watch her go by. I said to Michael that we would go down to Robin's Brae, so that's what we did.

May the 9th, 1981 was the day Queen Elizabeth the Second came to Shetland. Slim was on duty at the airport and it seemed that most of the population of the south of the island had gone there too. But as I said to Mike, she'd never spot us in that crowd and with only four other people waiting with us outside Geordie Mainland's shop, she couldn't miss us.

I had put on a warm duffel coat and, more especially, my home grown, hand spun, hand knitted hat. Nothing like flying the flag for Shetland. It was cold and we waited for what seemed like hours, then suddenly, whizzing round the corner came a shining, black, official car and right behind it, the one carrying the Queen. I waved madly and she, dear lady, graciously leaned forward, looked straight at us and waved back. True, it was the official royal wave but it was just for us, just for Michael and me. And then she was gone. The cars were travelling at speed for they were already behind schedule.

There is not much doubt that Her Majesty will not remember the funny little woman in a woolly hat who jumped up and down and waved with such enthusiasm, but it was a moment or two that will remain in my memory for a very long time.

When Slim came home that night he told us that the airport had been choc-a-bloc with people, so the decision to wait by the roadside had been a wise one. Discussing it later with Mimie she said that we had been luckier than she when another member of the Royal family had visited Shetland. He had landed at the airport to be driven to Lerwick. Mimie, with some friends, went to wait by the side of the road to see him pass by, but they got so deep in conversation that they forgot about him. It was not until someone asked what they were doing there that they discovered that His Royal Highness was long gone.

Visitors from afar were not often of such high rank. Family and friends constantly sought us out, no matter how remote we were.

'Why do you always live at the back of beyond?' I was once asked. Why indeed? Slim and I first lived in the wing of an isolated manor house a few miles from Fishguard in west Wales. From there we moved to Montrose in Scotland and thence to west Cornwall. In Cornwall we were swamped. A traditional holiday county, people we hadn't seen for years were suddenly keen to look us up. Friends and relations came from all quarters until I turned our bungalow into a bed and breakfast establishment and relegated them to the winter months.

Now that we had moved from one end of Great Britain to the other, and crossed water to do so, I didn't think many would want to venture that far. I was wrong. My brother came first while we were still living in the caravan and brought my Rayburn with him in the back of his Mini. My sister fled the west country when she became a widow and found solace and comfort in the peace and solitude of the islands. Now Slim's sister, husband and family were coming to stay with us.

Jan, her husband Remo and the boys, Taro and Cezar, lived in London. What on earth were city folk going to find to entertain them here? Only one cinema, no fancy restaurants, nothing for the kids. I needn't have worried, animals and children are a good mix.

There was a house full of small chickens to feed, to pick up and discover how soft their fluffy coats were. There were goats, there were calves. Lulu, Rusty and Dandy were always ready to be made a fuss of and had no objections to small arms being wrapped around their necks. There was an orphan lamb that had to be fed from a bottle. The boys were fascinated by the way she followed them round. They went fishing on the loch with Michael, caught two sea trout and had them for breakfast. Floss took to the boys like a duck to water.

Jan and Remo were keen to explore, but the boys were not and had almost to be frogmarched away from the croft. They visited more places during the few days they were with us than I had managed to do in all the time we had been here. They found a deserted fishing village in the north, thought they had been to Muckle Flugga and came home one day with a traffic cone.

'Look what we've got,' they said.

What on earth was I going to do with it?

'Just looking at the countryside doesn't really tell you much about it,' I said. 'I think you should meet some local people. Would you like me to ask some of our friends up for an evening?'

'That would be great,' they said.

John Henderson and Rosie, Jim Budge and Nancy, Jim and Greta Laurenson and Alex and Jessamine Smith braved the potholes of our track and made their way to Yawfield a couple of nights later. With Taro and Cezar safely tucked up in bed we settled down to enjoy the evening.

Our visitors were all good friends and with the lubrication of glasses of whisky the conversation flowed freely. Jan and Remo sat bemused, their heads turning first left and right as they listened to this one and that. It soon became obvious that they didn't understand a word of what was being said. John Henderson realised this and said to Jan in his best non-Shetland, 'You don't understand do you.'

'No,' said Jan. 'I don't.'

'Then I'll interpret for you,' said John and became self delegated interpreter for the evening. Afterwards Jan told me that she could understand some of what the others were saying and could understand John when he spoke directly to her, but when he spoke to the others she could understand nothing at all.

Regrettably Jan and Remo were unable to stay the course. After two whiskies Remo disappeared and we found him, sound asleep, spread-eagled on the bedroom floor, where he spent the rest of the night. Jan followed him soon after, climbed into bed, but was unable to shut the door because Remo was lying in the way. Sleep was to be denied her though. The route to the bathroom passed her door and traffic to it was quite regular.

'I don't know how you can sleep with all this noise going on,' was the comment made each time someone passed by. Of course it didn't help that dawn arrived some time before the party was over. Our friends departed in broad daylight. Our visitors left for home a few days later.

We always welcomed visitors to Yawfield, more so because they had to negotiate a rough and pitted track and to open and shut three gates that barred their way, not funny when it was raining. We had been south for a few days and had come back with a container of farmhouse cider. It was in a plastic barrel with a tap and had been left sitting on the worktop in the kitchen. It was still there when Mary and George came calling. George worked with Slim at the airport and he and Mary lived in a small township called Rerwick, just off the road to Sumburgh. Although there was not much room in the kitchen the Rayburn was alight and it was warm, so that was where we decided to sit.

'Have a glass of cider Mary,' said Slim.

'I don't know if I like it.'

'Well try some then.'

A glass was brought, held under the tap and half filled with the golden liquid. Mary took it and sipped tentatively. Her face lit up. 'It's nice,' she said, so we filled her glass. George was given a glass of cider too and Slim and I were not slow to follow them in filling glasses for ourselves. As the level in the glasses fell so the talk and laughter rose. Mary held out her empty glass and asked if she could have some more. 'Sure,' we said and topped up all round.

The kitchen was narrow so we sat in a row facing the worktop. The barrel of cider was in the middle facing us. Farmhouse cider is purely the juice of apples with nothing added. The natural yeasts that are present on the skin of, and in, the apple, are what makes it ferment and turn it into cider. As with wines there are good and bad years. The cider in our barrel was the product of a good year, was mellow and easy to drink. Mary thought so anyway for to my surprise I saw her put her glass under the tap of the barrel, turn it on and fill her glass again. I did not begrudge her but thought I should warn her of the potency of the liquid. 'Be careful Mary,' I said. 'It'll hit you later.' But she just smiled.

I felt obliged to ring her next morning to ask how she was.

'I'm all right now,' she said. 'But when we were coming home last night I had to get out to open the gate for George to drive through. When I shut it I discovered that I was one side and George was the other. I'd shut myself in.'

There were others who found that fermented apple juice is not as innocent as its name suggests.

When oil was discovered in the North Sea it brought many people to Shetland in search of work. After a year or two of inhospitable weather, lack of shopping facilities and conditions that were far less luxurious than most had been used to, many of them packed their bags and left. Jimmy and Wendy, our neighbours told us that they intended to move. They were not leaving Shetland though but going to Papa Stour, an island off the west coast. Papa had to be reached by boat and a small one at that. Wendy had become accomplished at knitting by machine and was to earn their living in the way many Shetlanders already did. We wondered who our new neighbours would be and what they would be like.

I met her in a café in Lerwick where I had gone for some lunch. As I was leaving a young woman stopped me and asked if I would give a message to Jimmy Milliken.

'My name is Luke,' she said. A girl called Luke? How very strange. When I gave Jimmy the message he told me that Luke was hoping to buy their house and if successful would be living there.

'She's a nice girl,' he said. 'She works at the airport.'

Luke bought Jimmy's house and moved in.

'Why did your parents name you Luke?' I asked.

'They didn't, but I was always called Luke so I had my name changed by deed poll.'

Luke was a vegetarian and cultivated the tiny garden round her house. In practice she had more success than I, but even so, gardening on that windswept hill was not easy. She was a good neighbour. She rode a motorbike which she left in a shed at Bobbie Mullay's old ruined croft house by the Maywick road. We heard her going off to work in the mornings, the sound of her bike carried loud and clear across to us. She too, preferred to use the road on the other side of the valley and walk home across the fields. The climb up the hill side was very steep, it needed young legs to tackle it. I would only walk up it if there was no other option.

The man from the Pru took a chance and almost became a fatality. We had seen him driving up from Maywick, stop his car, get out and look across. He stood for a while, obviously debating whether to drive the long way round or tackle the hill. It was one of those nice days in summer and the sunshine got the better of him. He left his car, got over the fence and made good time coming down the hill, then he disappeared from our sight when he reached the valley floor. I went inside to put the kettle on, he would surely like a cup of tea when he arrived.

The tea was made, the cups ready and the biscuit barrel on the table. He must be here now, I thought. I was about to go outside to see where he was when Slim came in at the door.

'Quick. Give me a glass of water Millie. I think the insurance man is having a heart attack.'

'He never is.'

'Well, he's lying on the grass and he's blue in the face.'

Poor man. He didn't have a heart attack, but he'd chosen the steepest part of the hill to climb, and, being unused to walking, it proved to be too much for him. They say that there is a reason for everything and in the case of the man from the Pru, it proved to be right. He went to his doctor and was told to lose weight and take more exercise. He took up hill walking in Scotland.

CHAPTER FIFTEEN

The airport at Sumburgh where Luke and Slim both worked was little more than a collection of wooden huts. The traffic of men going to and from the rigs stretched what facilities there were to the limits. New hangars had been erected to house the aircraft. Plans had been drawn up for a modern terminal to be built on the eastern side of the runways. A new road would have to be built and a small hill levelled. Work went ahead. There was much debate as to the necessity of it all. Many thought the new terminal would be a white elephant and a millstone round the neck.

In a landscape that had changed so very little during the preceding years a modern building was to be erected. It would contrast strangely with the granite edifice that was the Sumburgh Hotel, once a laird's house. That too had suffered the indignity of having temporary accommodation tacked on to it to provide bedrooms for transient workers.

Times, they were a-changing.

In spite of its shortcomings, the old terminal was a welcome sight on landing at the airport. It was cosy and informal and walking into it was like coming home. Slim was qualified to work on fixed wing aircraft as well as helicopters and was the engineer for the British Airways domestic flights. Always a softie where small children were concerned he dressed in his Santa

Claus outfit to guide the aircraft in on Christmas Eve and had a packet of sweets for each child on board in his pocket.

We had been in Shetland for six years. Michael was now a boarder at the Anderson High School in Lerwick. He was away from home all week and with Slim working long days I had many hours to fill. Floss was my constant companion, we were always together. I had trained her to work with the sheep, to round them up and bring them to me and to pick out and separate any that needed attention. There was always something to do.

Lulu had grown into a good-looking animal and was old enough to be put in calf. I had been told that artificial insemination was not very successful in Shetland. Whether that was because of the time lapse in getting the inseminator to the cow or for any other reason was not clear. The usual practice was to take the cow to the bull. Jim Budge was the nearest farmer who kept a bull so we asked him if Lulu could pay a visit. The answer was yes, so we borrowed a trailer and took her to the farm. A few days later Jim phoned to say that she was ready to come home. Now all we could do was to cross our fingers and hope for the best. Success was not guaranteed.

Being out of doors in the cold air a lot gave us all healthy appetites. We had already savoured the delights of reestit mutton soup, Mimie's clootie dumplings and Bella's bannocks, among other things, when we tried a haggis. Made from mutton, oatmeal, onions, pepper and salt and a sheep's pluck, it was a very tasty dish. Haggis is not unlike the faggots we had at home, the difference being that faggots are made with pigs' liver. Always keen to try something new I intended to make a haggis the next time we killed a sheep.

When the time came, I gave instructions for the stomach bag to be saved for me. Getting out my cookery book I began to follow the instructions. "Wash the stomach bag in cold water and salt." I did that. Turned it inside out and tried to scrape off the green stain on the inside. I didn't fancy my haggis flavoured with grass. I scraped and scraped, then gave up when I thought the bag was getting too thin. "Boil pluck, leaving windpipe hanging out of pot...." I won't go into detail here but I followed the directions word for word – I think – then put the resulting haggis in a pot to boil. Three or four hours they said it would take so I had plenty of time to go out and feed the sheep and off I went.

I always used to think that any fool could cook. If they could read they could follow the directions in a cookery book, so how could they go wrong? I take it all back. When I returned from feeding my animals I homed in on a very pleasant aroma coming from the kitchen. My haggis must be doing well. I divested myself of boots, hat and anorak, went to the cooker and lifted the lid of the saucepan. The sight that met my eyes was not as I had expected. Instead of a tight round ball sitting in the middle of its surrounding waters I saw what looked like a very thick soup. Then the skin of the stomach bag surfaced. Bloop, bloop it went and then sank. It surfaced again... and bloop, bloop it went before it disappeared once more under a morass of onion, oatmeal and goodness knows what else.

A haggis I hadn't got, but what I had, was a pot full of something very tasty.

I wasn't about to throw it away so I got some vegetables, cut them up and added them to the pot, in fact I divided it all up and made two pots of it. We were eating haggis stew for the best part of a week.

'It's that time of year again.'

'What time is that?'

'It's time to cut the peat.'

I groaned inwardly. I knew what that meant. Slim would say next that I should go up and skim the surface so that he could do the hard work of actually digging the peat. We had done it before but our peat stack never assumed the proportions we saw stacked so neatly outside just about every house in the neighbourhood.

However, the next day that I could find nothing more important to do I set off in the direction of our peat bank. We had bought a tushkar but it and a peat barrow was the sum total of our peat casting tools. To flay the tough heathery surface from off the layer of peat I took with me a Cornish shovel. The blade of it was quite literally the same shape as a spade on a pack of cards. The soil in Cornwall is thin and rocky and the point of the spade was the best thing to use to pierce the surface. It was not the best thing for skimming off the turf but I hacked, sweated and swore and stopped frequently to drink coffee from my flask.

It was done at last, or at least as much as I was going to struggle with that day. I sat down in the heather to rest and now that work no longer claimed my attention I was able to direct it to my surroundings.

It was one of those rare days when the sun shines and the sky is blue and Shetland smiles on all around. From wide horizons the arc of the sky was vast. Lifting my head I gazed into infinity. Birds wheeled and floated on currents of air high above, the thin sound of their cries drifting down to me.

A few hundred yards from where I sat the cliff edge plunged down to meet the waters of the Atlantic. I could hear the grumble of the waves as they threw themselves at the unyielding rock face. Though they may peck at it here and there the old rock will stand resolute for a good many years yet.

Turning to look toward Foula I saw a fishing boat ploughing through the waves. Up she would rise to ride the crest then sink into a trough until only the top of her wheelhouse was visible, then up she would come again. As she proceeded a cloud of seagulls flew above her, obviously a catch was being cleaned for they dived and circled, watching for a tit-bit to be thrown overboard.

I got up from my couch on the heather to ramble over the moor. I found the common butterwort trying to hide in the wiry grass. It looks very similar to the violets that grow in the hedgerows 'doon sooth'. In one spot I heard the chuckling of water running beneath the heather, I tried to follow it to see where it came into the open but it must have dived underground for I never found beginning nor end.

With a couple of days off work Slim said he was going to cut our peat. We put the tushkar and the spade in the barrow, along with a flask of coffee and some sandwiches and were off. We were accompanied by Floss and, so that they could enjoy a change of scenery, a couple of goats.

While Slim cut the peat I helped lay them on the bank. We were not very good at it and I was glad we were on the side of the hill away from the people of the village for their peat was laid up in very neat formation. I followed the example of the locals and went frequently to turn our peat to dry and cure in the wind. Later I went to stack them in a larger pile and finally to report that they were ready to bring home.

We were not able to get close to our peats with the tractor and trailer so the peat barrow was brought into use. We had bought it at a sale and now it was going to come into its own. The bottom and sides were made of strips of wood so that it was very light and easy to handle. Sacks were filled with peat and were then loaded on to the barrow. With Slim taking the handles and Michael or I pulling on a rope attached to the front we negotiated the humps and bumps to the tractor. Back and forth we went until the trailer was full. Three times we filled it, goodness only knows how many times we fought our way from peat bank to trailer.

Outside Mimie's house was a peat stack that was a work of art. She told me how it was built. The outer edge was constructed of slabs of peat which sloped gently inward. The smaller and broken peats filled the middle. On the top were slabs of turf placed at such an angle that rain would run off and not penetrate the stack. Not for us a neat stack of peat though. I'm ashamed to say we threw them willy-nilly into one of the outhouses, there to stay until we needed them.

When winter came and the wind blew cold we lit the fire. A basket of peats was brought in. Paper and wood laid in the grate and a match struck. For a while the fire crackled and the flames danced merrily. But then the burning peats settled down to a rosy glow and a thin column of smoke rose up the chimney. I thought of Bobbie Smith and his comments on peat.

'You'll get warm digging them, warm getting them home, but not very warm by the fire.'

Oh for a fire of sweet smelling apple logs. Just then came a down draught and the chimney belched a cloud of acrid smoke into our faces, making us cough.

'Lang may your lum reek,' someone had said, just then I wished mine did not.

With the peats cut and carried the next work of the croft was to harvest the wool from the sheep's backs. After my first attempt at shearing and when I realised I was going to have to do it again, and to several more sheep, I thought it would be wise to seek advice. My neighbours were clipping their sheep so I went along to watch. I asked innumerable questions and learned that young sheep were sheared before the old ones.

Meeting up with neighbours was always a social occasion and a cup of tea or a dram frequently offered. I was on my way home from Lerwick one day and didn't fancy the thought of going home once more to an empty house, I'd go and visit somebody. When I thought about it some more I realised there was nobody I could go to, all my friends would be at work. I'd go and walk on Maywick sands then, that would be a fine thing to do.

Cruising down the Maywick road I happened upon Bobbie Mullay and another man. They had sheep penned and were busy clipping. I parked the van and got out to talk to them.

'This is my brother, Alec,' said Bobbie, and to Alec, 'and this is Millie, she lives at Yawfield.'

Alec held out a hand well lubricated with lanolin off the sheep, I took it and we shook hands. He climbed out of the pen and went to his jacket which was hanging on a post. Taking a half bottle out of a pocket he unscrewed the top, gave it a quick rub with his hand then offered it to me.

'Will you take a dram?' he said.

I hesitated, no doubt he'd transferred more germs on to the bottle than he'd removed. 'It's a bit early for me,' I said.

'Ah, go on. I've only just met you.'

'Oh well, why not.' I took the bottle, put it to my mouth, took a draught and swallowed. It was neat, it was strong and it was good. I smiled as I handed back the bottle. 'Cheers,' I said.

I stayed a while to watch them as they worked and exchanged gossip before deciding it was time to go. I drove down to the bottom of the road, turned the van and headed for home. When I got there I changed my clothes, rounded up my sheep and made a start on stealing their fleece. I'm not sure whether it was pure enthusiasm or the whisky in my blood which gave impetus to my arm, but within the space of an hour I had denuded ten of them.

The native Shetland sheep are the easiest to shear. When the new season's wool starts to grow and the old lifts off there is a yellow line of droplets of lanolin oil making a dividing line between the two. I was told that it was called the yolk. The oil from a sheep's wool saturates every stitch of clothing and penetrates the skin. It has a very softening effect and is probably the reason it is used in cosmetics.

Crossbred sheep are much more difficult to clip, especially for a novice. The wool is more dense and does not rise. The sheep themselves are thicker set and heavier which also makes for harder work.

July and August are Shetland's summer months. Not every day is hot and sunny but usually the rain holds off. Sometimes a warm summer day will draw the mist inland off the sea. One day I watched as the mist came in over the hill and, starting as a small cloud, ran a long finger down the hill side. Reaching the valley floor it spread out to fill it, then came swirling towards us to surround us with a cold and penetrating damp. All around was white and wet. Summer had been cancelled for the day.

The turf of much of Shetland is old, tundra Slim calls it. It is the home of millions of midges and when conditions are right they come out in force. On such a day it is not wise to venture forth. Slim is impervious to biting insects and flies, he has something called an enzyme in his skin and mosquitos or midges that dare to bite him are doomed to die.

But midges are purgatory for me, they swarm about my eyes, my ears, creep down the neck of my blouse and attack any portion of my skin that is exposed. I have to admit defeat and retire to the safety of the house.

The islands of Shetland, scattered at random in the North Sea are at the mercy of every wind that blows. Soft breezes from the south, keen, cold winds from the east. Icy, snow bearing winds from every quarter. There are mists and fogs, dull days and cold days. Winter is long and dreary, summer days nearly twenty-four hours long and summer is over too soon.

But there comes a day when the weather is perfect. The rain stops, the winds cease to blow, the skies clear and Shetland smiles and shows us how beautiful she really is. Weather is so important that it is no wonder that the rare perfect day is known as 'a day between weathers'.

As summer dies autumn brings a bout of nostalgia. I dream of the golden days home in the south of England, when the leaves drift like confetti off the trees, where apples lie and rot in the long grass of the orchard and the harvest is over and safely in the barn.

Nothing but the dark days of winter lie before me now. These are sad days. Though autumn is not the same in the islands I still suffer the melancholy and at this time my homesickness is most acute.

September brings migrating birds passing through on their way to warmer climes. Our hill side was bare and windswept and not many birds made landfall there. For us the first hint that migration was under way was the sound of the geese. As they flew overhead on their way to their resting places we could hear them honking. No matter what I was doing, to hear them sent me running outside to look up and wish that when they went south I could go with them.

They stayed at several places in the south of the mainland, across the hill to the east of us at Levenwick and Clumlie, and south of us at Ireland. They only stayed a short while to rest and regain their strength before continuing their journey south and one day when we looked for them they would be gone.

At home alone, working at something or other inside the house I heard the geese. Dropping what I was doing I rushed outside. There they were. A gaggle of large grey birds. But something was wrong. They were flying north and for September it was not the way to go.

As I watched them they banked right and flew east and as they did I saw a cloud of birds rising from the other side of the hill. Up they went and merged with the first group. Changing course again they all turned toward the south and from the Clumlie area more geese rose up. By now the gaggle had turned into a large black cloud. They would be heading south for certain now, I thought. I rushed inside to get the binoculars so that I could watch them go.

Outside again I focussed on the geese. They were still turning right, flying west and then north again. They flew quite low. I could see them clearly. Straight toward me and right above me they came, I could hear the rush of their wings beating the air, the sound mixed with their incessant gabbling. Head and neck straight and stiff, feet and legs tucked in and streamlined beneath the tail feathers. Their ponderous bodies were carried effortlessly along by the slow, strong beat of their wings. So close were they to me I could see every detail of their markings.

Their flight path turned eastward once more and finally, rising higher as they flew, they headed south. I put the binoculars to my eyes and watched as they arranged themselves into the familiar V formation. I stood there and wished that I too could spread my wings and fly away with them. They were going and I had to stay. I carried a heavy heart round with me for the rest of the day.

It was hard to feel sad for too long when Slim was around though. His quick wit and lively sense of humour could coax a smile from the most woebegone face. His general knowledge was excellent. Sometimes when I was quite sure of my facts on a particular point he would prove me wrong.

'You know I'm always right,' he would say.

One day in desperation, at having been proved wrong yet again, I snapped.

'It's wonder you don't suffer from headaches,' I muttered.

'And why would that be?'

'Because your head is so big your halo must surely pinch at times.'

Slim just laughed but Michael thought it was extremely funny.

'Why don't we make him a halo, Mum?' he suggested.

The idea appealed to me so we found a length of soft wire, twisted one end into a circle, which we judged would fit Slim's head, left a straight length of about four inches and twisted the remaining length of wire into a circle as before. The wire was then adjusted so that the two circles were one above the other, the top one being held there by the straight piece. A piece of silver tinsel, filched from the Christmas decoration box, was wound round one of the circles and the halo was complete.

We presented it to Slim who said, 'Thank you. I've always wanted one of these.' He wore it for a while and put it on the shelf in the porch when he had to go out. Unfortunately it got knocked on to the floor and, even more unfortunately Slim stepped one of the circles of wire, caught his toe in the other and before I could shout a warning, fell flat on his face. His halo had tripped him up.

Laughter comes easily in our house. Michael and I rolled on the floor, convulsed in a paroxysm of mirth and laughed until the tears rolled down our cheeks and our sides ached.

The laughter had to stop though when Slim came home from work and said, 'There's a rumour going round that British Airways Helicopters are going to get Chinooks for Aberdeen.'

'What about it?'

'It means that if they do Sumburgh will become redundant and will not be flying oilies out to the rigs.'

'And how is that going to affect us?'

'We can either move to Aberdeen with the company or stay here.'

This could not be. We had been assured by BA that the work in Shetland would last a very long time. I thought about it for a while.

'And what do you want to do?' I asked Slim.

'Stay here.'

Stay here. I wondered how we would manage for work if British Airways moved away. Would there be a job for Michael when he left school? I could see that the tide was beginning to turn and work was going to get scarce. It was no use worrying about something that might yet be nothing more than a rumour, but the seeds of doubt had been sown and from time to time worry niggled at my brain.

There was nothing to be done about it though so as winter approached I continued to walk out to inspect my sheep, continued to look at Lulu and wonder if she was carrying a calf and continued to do all the day to day work that a home and croft required.

CHAPTER SIXTEEN

'It's official. British Airways are getting Chinooks at Aberdeen. The landing fees are so high at Sumburgh it is too expensive to land there so it is going to be by-passed. The new terminal is the white elephant that everyone said it would be. They didn't need to build such a fancy place. They could have vamped up the old terminal, it would have been cheaper, much more viable and convenient.'

I stood still, open mouthed and aghast. Not often did Slim make such an outburst as this. But now our future was in the balance. We had been given to expect that there was security in the work situation at the airport and now it was being cut from under our feet. I must admit that part of me wanted to move even though Slim had made it clear he wanted to stay.

As the years had passed I was finding that working with the sheep, going out in all weathers to feed and see to them was getting harder. I had had enough of hard work and as I was getting older I thought it was time I retired. We had moved our living quarters to the four corners of Great Britain while Slim was in the Navy and several times since he had left it. At every move we had bought properties that needed doing up and we had lived in what might virtually be called building sites for too long. All I dreamed of now was a small house with a garage and a patch of garden. No animals, no land, time to spare and time for the things I wanted to do, like embroidery and knitting. I wanted to be just a housewife again.

'What are we going to do then Millie? Go or stay?'

'I don't think it's up to me. We ought to discuss it more and make a joint decision. If we stay what will there be for us here? Will there still be a job at the airport for you? What is Michael going to do? Every time he goes for an interview a Shetland boy gets the job. That's the way it should be of course because it's their home, but where does that leave Mike?'

The questions came thick and fast. We made endless cups of tea and talked well into the night, but time after time came up with no answers.

If we moved to Aberdeen with the company they would pay our removal expenses. If we stayed behind and could not find work and it was no longer practical to stay then we would have the burden of the expense of moving ourselves. It was likely to cost in the region of two thousand pounds.

If we decided to go we would have to sell the croft. They were not usually sold but handed down from parents to children or sometimes assigned to another person. If we were going to sell, where were we going to find a buyer? Local opinion was that we wouldn't be able to sell. We seemed to be in a desperate situation.

Finally, and after much deliberation, the move to Aberdeen was accepted as being the logical conclusion to our dilemma. We placed an advertisement in the *Telegraph*, offering the house and land, got a reply from Scandinavia, but no sale.

We had hoped that the wider circulation of a national newspaper might find the person we were looking for. Weeks went by in which we were in a state of flux, not knowing which way to go. Then we decided to try the *Shetland Times*. A few people were interested, one young couple in particular, but they had young children and thought it too isolated for them. It seemed as though we had come to a full stop again.

The postmark on the letter was Leeds. I looked at the unfamiliar handwriting and continued to stand with the letter in my hand and wonder who it could be from.

'Slim, who do we know in Leeds?' I said, waving the letter under his nose.

'Why d'you stand there looking at it? Why don't you open the envelope and find out?'

We didn't know the person who had written to us. It was in fact an exiled Shetlander who was interested in coming home to live and was asking for particulars of the croft. I put together the details and without wasting any more time got them into the letterbox. Almost by return came a request for an appointment for the enquirer to come and view.

Mr Gilbertson brought his mother with him. She was a little white haired old lady and if he bought the croft she would be coming there to live with him.

'Is it really the right place to bring her?' we asked. 'If you are away at work all day she will be alone for a very long time.'

'She was born and bred in Shetland,' he said. 'She'll be used to it.'

Well, it was his choice. We walked the fields to point out the boundaries, showed him the flock of sheep that was included in the sale, looked over the machinery that was also included and explained the workings of the poultry business. He was interested but said he had another place to view. Oh dear. We had better keep our fingers crossed.

A few days later Mr Gilbertson phoned to ask for another appointment to discuss the property. He came alone this time. He was interested in the place, he said, and wanted to buy. We asked him again if he thought it was the right place for his mother, but he brushed aside our worries and before he left us said he would buy the croft.

So the place was sold. There would be no waiting and worrying lest anything go wrong before contracts were signed. In Scottish law the words, 'I will buy,' constitutes a binding contract. All we had to do now was to agree a completion date and wait for the legal papers to be drawn up.

We were on the move again. The period of time between selling one property and buying the next is a time of uncertainty. We bought the *Press and Journal*, an Aberdeen based newspaper, for its property supplement. Scanning through it we rapidly came to the conclusion that houses in that area were vastly more expensive than comparative properties in Shetland. Aberdeen had been affected by the oil boom to a much greater degree than Shetland. All the oil companies, Shell, B.P. etcetera had bases there. There were many oil related industries in the area and the price of property had rocketed. We took time off to go to Aberdeen to see what we could get for our money.

We looked at the houses in and around the city, but having lived with plenty of elbow room for so long the thought of having neighbours breathing down our necks filled us with dread. We travelled out to the surrounding countryside and found that quite small bungalows were selling for fifty thousand pounds. Neighbours were not quite as close but still not more than a few hundred yards away.

'I don't think it's a good idea to buy a house Millie,' said Slim. 'The boom will fall off here like it has in Shetland and the price of property will drop. We would lose money.'

'What are we going to do then? We have to live somewhere.'

'We'd better get another farm.'

'*What?*'

'Land maintains its value. Houses don't.'

He was right of course, and having acknowledged that, I saw my dream of retirement begin to fade. Once Slim has made up his mind about something it is very hard to try to get him to change it, so, we continued to look at the property gazette, but now we were looking at the agricultural section. The price being asked for farms was lower by comparison than that being asked for houses. For fifty thousand it was possible to buy a farmhouse with a range of outbuildings and sixty or seventy acres of land. It would need capital to stock it but it could provide a living.

'Here's a place just outside Ellon. A farm with ninety acres.'

'Isn't that too big for us?'

'We could always rent the grazing. How far is it from the airport?'

On the map we had drawn a circle round the airport and agreed that we would have to find a property within its boundaries. The distance to the perimeter of the circle was about twenty miles. We thought it should be the limit of Slim's journey to work. The farm advertised was just on the edge of the circle. We liked the description of the place so sent away for more details. When we received them we liked the sound of them even more so decided to travel down to view it.

We flew to Aberdeen and rented a car. Driving north we passed through the small town of Ellon and, following the scanty directions we had been given, turned off the main road. The address was Mosshead of Dudwick. We thought that Dudwick must be a village.

The area was not thickly populated. A farm here and there with a small house, the bedroom windows protruding from the roof like frog's eyes. The buildings were of granite with roofs of slate. Cottages were built of granite too. We drove on expecting to find a signpost directing us to Dudwick, but we found none.

Rather than drive round in circles we stopped at a small village to ask the way and found we were not far from our destination. A left turn and then a right and we'd find it on the top of the hill. We turned left and right and began a long steady climb. We passed a tumbledown cottage and a little further on a derelict croft and buildings.

Another croft house, with a few stone outbuildings and an old railway carriage beside it sat looking down the hill. The signpost by its entrance told us that it was called Little Mains of Dudwick. We must be close to Mosshead now.

We drove on up the hill. At the very top there was a huge barn which didn't seem to be in use. Weatherboards were hanging off it and I could imagine the wind playing havoc with it when a gale was blowing. The road dipped and we passed another deserted cottage. Rising once more to the crest of the hill we found the entrance to the farm. The roadway climbed a few more feet, then we were over the top and as we began the descent we could see the farm laid out before us.

The house was as other farmhouses we had seen. Squat and square, built of granite and slate. Beyond it were some fairly modern buildings. To the left, a long low wooden hut. As we reached the house the farmer came out to greet us. He wore a tweed coat and jeans and on his head a tartan cap with a bobble on top. When he shook my hand the palm of his was hard and tough.

'How do you do, Mr Cheyne,' I said.

'My name's Sandy, you can call me that. Everyone else does.'

Sandy shook Slim by the hand too then invited us in for a cup of tea and to meet his wife. Mrs Cheyne was a little lady. She sat in a chair by a Rayburn that was going full blast. Sandy made us tea and we exchanged small talk while we drank it. Then he showed us over the house.

There were two bedrooms and a box room upstairs, a sitting room, bathroom and kitchen on the ground floor. There was also a small room in a lean-to where things like egg boxes, milk cans and other oddments were left.

The farm buildings had been partly modernised. There were two large silage pits, a cattle court, byre and machinery shed. The large wooden building contained pig pens but no pigs. To inspect the fields Sandy drove us round in his car. All sorts of things had been thrown into it. Tools, sacks, empty oil cans. A layer of dust and dog hairs covered everything. In deference to my clean clothes Sandy thumped the passenger seat but only made the dust fly. He apologised for it and invited me to climb in.

Sandy had worked hard during the time he had owned the farm and had won good ground from a stony, heather clad hill. He and his wife had moved tons of stone, he said, there was not a field in Aberdeenshire that did not contain lumps of granite. The round of inspection completed we thanked him for showing us his farm and said we'd let him know of our decision.

'I hope you have it Mistress,' he said to me. 'You're a hard working woman.'

I was wearing my best clothes and didn't think I looked like a farmer that day so I said, 'And what makes you think that?'

'By your hands lassie, by your hands.'

Well, yes they weren't lily white, and they didn't have red talons an inch long, and there was a callous or two on the palm, so I suppose it was they that gave me away.

We put in our offer, it was accepted and when all formalities were complete arrangements were made for us to take possession of it in October of that year. Slim had already put in an application to move with British Airways to Aberdeen but paper work takes a long time and it took weeks to sort it all out.

Mimie had been very sad to hear that we were leaving. I too was sorry to leave her for she had been a very good friend to me. In fact it would be a wrench to leave all our friends. They had been so kind in their welcome and if they thought we were completely mad to buy the house at Yawfield, they never criticised what we did or made us feel they were laughing at us behind our backs. We had tried to adapt to their way of life and though some of the things they did seemed to belong to the past, there were some very good reasons for doing them the way they did.

It was time to start sorting through the contents of the house. I hated throwing things away for as soon as they were gone they were needed, but something had to go. Once again my home was to be stowed away in boxes and it had not been long since I had rediscovered items packed before we left Cornwall.

Our farm machinery had been sold with the croft, it would not have been practical to take it with us. We would need implements to work the new farm so Slim planned to go to the farm sale at Mosshead to buy what he could of Sandy's machinery. Michael was to go with him. Sandy had invited them to stay at the farm overnight to be in time for the sale in the morning.

I drove them to the airport and watched as the plane took off in the morning. As it climbed away into the sky I wondered if Michael had remembered his inhaler. When I got home again there it was lying on the desk. I hoped he wouldn't have an attack of asthma but was pretty certain that he would. There was nothing I could do however, and as I knew Slim was capable of coping with an emergency there was no point in worrying.

The next twenty-four hours dragged interminably and I was at the airport long before the plane that was bringing them home was due to land. At last it came winging in over the lighthouse at Sumburgh Head. When I saw them walking across the tarmac to me they were happy and smiling. A good omen.

'How did you get on then? What did you buy?'

'Later, I'll tell you later,' said Slim. 'You'll never believe what happened and you'll die laughing when I tell you.'

'But did you buy anything?'

'Oh yes. We got a tractor, a trailer, lots of things. I've got a list, I'll give it to you when we get home.'

I drove away from the airport, up over Wart Hill and when we were on the straight road at the top I asked what had happened that had been so funny.

'When we got to the airport, Sandy was there to meet us, but there was another man with him.' Slim chuckled. 'We went out of the terminal building expecting to get into Sandy's car but instead we got into a taxi.' He laughed now. 'The other man was a taxi driver. Sandy didn't know how to get to the airport so he had driven into Aberdeen, parked his car and got a taxi.'

'Well, that was the first thing. We got to the farm and Sandy showed us round. We looked at all the implements and decided which ones we should try to buy. When it was time for bed Sandy showed us to our room. The bed was one of those old Victorian ones with brass knobs. When we pulled back the covers we found there were no sheets, just blankets, you know how they make you itch. Michael got in first and promptly rolled into the middle.' Both Slim and Michael were laughing now.

'The springs had no guts so the bed sagged. I got in and rolled on top of Michael, thought I was going to suffocate him. It was awful. Then in the middle of the night Michael got asthma, he'd forgotten his inhaler. He was hoping it would go away, but it didn't so he woke me. We had to get up and wake Sandy then. Went to his bedroom door and knocked.'

All the time Slim was telling his tale he chuckled and laughed and Michael was laughing too, their laughter was infectious and I was laughing as well. But there was more to come.

'The door opened and there was Sandy. He was wearing his bobble cap and COMBINATIONS! He looked like a miniature cowboy out of a John Wayne movie. I don't know how I didn't laugh in his face.'

Michael broke in. 'I could hardly breathe, Mum, but I had to turn away so that he wouldn't see me laughing.' He laughed again at the memory. Slim was laughing and I was laughing too, so much that my sides were aching.

But Sandy was a trooper, he got dressed, phoned the doctor and arranged to take them both to meet him at the surgery in Ellon.

'He drove like a maniac,' Slim recalled. 'Took the first turning too fast, missed a telegraph pole by the skin of his teeth, got to Ellon and drove down a one way street the wrong way. "There's no-one about at this time of night," he said, and we reached the surgery. Michael got a new inhaler and in a little while he was all right again, so back we went to the farm and back to bed.'

The telling was liberally accompanied by chuckles from Michael and hoots of laughter from Slim. I thought that was all.

'There's more,' said Slim and went off into another fit of laughter. 'In the morning Sandy made breakfast. In a huge frying pan he cooked thick rashers of bacon, put them in the oven to keep warm while he fried eggs. Eggs, eggs, eggs. He just kept on cracking eggs until the pan was full. There were duck eggs, hen eggs and bantam's eggs, must have been at least a dozen. Plates were set down in front of us and Sandy dished up the bacon. It was thick and greasy. Then came the eggs. Some on his plate, some on Michael's and some on... whoops, missed... some on the table. He put down the pan, picked up my plate and with his hand, very neatly swept the eggs on to it.'

Slim laughed at the memory but it had made Michael feel ill so he'd pleaded an onset of asthma again, left his breakfast and escaped.

'What did you do, Slim?' I asked.

'I've eaten all sorts of strange food in different parts of the world, I wasn't going to offend the man so I ate it.'

Having survived the night and the event of breakfast it was time to meet the auctioneers and some of the local people. Sandy Cheyne was well known so farmers and their wives from a wide area came to the sale. Some of those who would be our new neighbours were introduced to Slim, no doubt they looked him up and down and wondered what sort of a man he was. The barn had been given over to a bar where whisky and beer flowed freely, there were also sandwiches and pies to eat.

The last few weeks before the date of our leaving were hectic. Estimates of removal expenses were sought and Pickfords chosen. We were taking the cattle, some lambs and a goat with us so transport to the quayside and accommodation for them on the boat was arranged and cabins booked for us.

Boxes in which to pack our things came from the removal firm. There was also a cat box, very neat and in the shape of a little house. How considerate. We were told that if we collected all the small items together, such as crockery, glass and ornaments, the carrier's men would pack them either the day before or on the morning of the move.

Like many other women I was not keen to let strangers handle my personal belongings, so having had several experiences of moving house I set about packing them myself. There must be a way to move house and remain sane but if there is I haven't found it yet. As soon as a box was packed and labelled I found there was something in it that was desperately needed, so packing and unpacking became my main occupation until finally I abandoned all hope of ever being ready in time to catch the boat.

And then to top it all Slim suggested we should have a farewell party.

'Do you want them to come in relays then?' I asked. 'There isn't room enough here for all the people I'd want to invite.'

'How much do you think it would cost to book the hall at Bigton?'

'I've no idea. Shall I ring Willie Tait and find out?'

'Do that.'

Willie didn't tell me what the fee would be but said that it wouldn't be very much. So a date was agreed and the hall booked.

CHAPTER SEVENTEEN

Slim handed over the organisation of the party to me. 'You're good at that sort of thing,' he said. There was no list of invitations to write for there was no-one I'd wish to exclude. Instead I made a poster which was displayed in the window of the shop at Bigton. It was an open invitation to anyone in the neighbourhood to come to our farewell party at the village hall.

'How many do you think I'll have to cater for Slim?'

'Could be anything from one to two hundred.'

'So what shall I do about food? D'you think a buffet would be the best thing? I could get it all ready beforehand and I'll only need to ask one or two to help with the washing up.'

It was agreed that a buffet would be just the thing. A bar licence was obtained and the services of a local dance band booked. I made shopping lists, borrowed a cake tray to make a trifle in, cooked beef and ham, sausages and quiche. I sliced tomatoes and cucumbers and washed lettuce, made Waldorf Salad and savoury rice and buttered piles of bread.

At last everything was ready, packed in the van and carried to the hall. I checked it over to make sure nothing was forgotten, hoped someone would turn up to eat it all, then turning the key in the door went home to change.

The three of us, bathed and clean, smelling of talcum powder, after shave and perfume as a change from the smell of sheep and cattle, got into the Renault and set off down the track.

Slim and I stood at the doorway of the hall to greet our guests. Mimie and her family, Laurence, June and the twins, Colin and Allen were among the first to arrive. Willie Leask came, and his daughter Edna of the big dark eyes. Elma from across the valley was there, Alec Smith and Jim Burgess, Slim's workmates, Angela from the straight mile, silky blonde hair and small round face. They came and many others, all of them our friends.

The band arrived and set themselves up on the stage. The bar was open for drinks. A good number of people had already come along and more were to come later. The band struck up and dancing began.

Shetlanders do not do things by halves, when they dance it is with lots of enthusiasm and enjoyment. Colin insisted I do the eightsome reel with him. We bobbed and curtsied and twirled but my ability didn't match his. I lost my grip and with it my balance and went crashing to the floor to skid, very inelegantly, among the other dancers' feet. Bumps and spills were all part of the fun though and a dram of whisky deadened the pain most admirably.

With no shortage of partners I danced until the soles of my feet grew hot and I was glad when I heard Slim say that it was time for some food. I don't think I was the only one to be glad of a respite, a chance to cool off and draw breath.

The helpers who had so kindly offered to assist with the buffet were very efficient. Trestle tables were set up, covered with cloths and the food brought out. There was plenty for all. Slim was so afraid that it might run out before everyone was fed that there was an excess.

'I know now why Slim is not,' said Willie Tait, grinning at me as he filled his own plate.

Refreshments over, my helpers, Elma, Greta, Julia, Mimie and others, worked rapidly to clear the debris. We were then able to return to the dance floor where, to my surprise, I saw Slim skipping lightly through yet another reel. The party went on, a room full of happy people dancing away the night. When the hour was getting late Slim called the party to order.

'We have a little present for you,' he said, and calling Willie Tait over to him, gave him a hammer and a nail saying, 'Go over to that wall and I'll tell you where to bang it in.'

Willie's face wore a look of puzzlement. Why on earth did he have to hammer a nail in the wall? Teasing him, Slim sent him right and left until he finally said, 'That's all right. Bang it in there.'

When the nail was fixed Slim handed Willie a box. 'Now hang the contents on the nail,' he directed. The box contained a clock. 'And that's a thank you for all the happy hours we've spent with you all,' he concluded.

It was our turn then to receive a 'thank you' for the party. I was presented with a lovely bouquet of flowers by Edna Leask. A going away present from Angela Henderson and for Slim, a wallet from Willie Leask that had been generously filled by many of Slim's friends.

Hands came then, took my flowers and gift and lifted me high on strong shoulders. I looked down on a sea of smiling faces. I think someone managed to get Slim's feet off the floor too.

The party had been a success but, now that it was over, the time we had left on Shetland was rapidly growing short. It was October, the geese were long gone and soon we would be heading south as well. Now that the time had actually come, happiness and sadness were inextricably mixed. We visited Mimie to say goodbye, hugged her long and tight and promised to come back as soon and as often as possible. Then it was back again to the packing and clearing up.

The day before we were due to sail the man from Pickfords came to start packing the boxes. As I watched him deftly wrapping, packing and protecting one fragile piece from another I was glad I had left the china and glass to him. At the end of the day all the boxes had been filled.

'There you are my dear,' he said as he put his coat on. 'The lorry will be with you about eight thirty in the morning.'

We listened to the weather forecast on Shetland Radio that evening. A northerly gale was imminent. We didn't think about the ferry coming up from Aberdeen, only that it might mean a quick passage south.

We were tired that night and slept well. When we woke in the morning it was to hear the wind whistling about the house. The gale was with us. It was still early when Andy Flaws drove up with his lorry to take Lulu and the rest of the animals to the dock.

'The boat'll be late this morning. The gale will hold it back,' he said.

'Not too late I hope, our stuff has to be packed into the lorry and we have to get to Lerwick at least an hour before it sails again.'

'You're going to have to work fast then,' was all he would say.

We loaded our stock into his lorry and he drove off with them. There was nothing we could do now but have a look round to see if there was anything we'd missed that should have been packed.

Eight thirty came and went and there was no sign of Pickford's lorry. Nine o'clock saw us driving up to the top of the hill to see if it was anywhere in sight. The hands on the clock moved past nine-thirty and crept toward ten. It altered nothing to worry and wonder what had happened but we did all the same.

'Look, look. There's the lorry on the Maywick road.'

There was only one wrong turning the lorry driver could have taken... and he had. We saw the lorry rolling down the Maywick road and knew that it would have to go all the way to the bottom before it could turn round and come back. It was ten thirty now, it would be almost another hour before it could get to us. We were supposed to be on the quayside and ready to be loaded by two thirty. We'd never make it. What would happen to the animals if we couldn't get there in time?

At long last the removal lorry was backed up to the door of the house, the tailboard let down and loading started. The driver would not allow a stop for tea. I tried to help but only succeeded in getting in the way. I wanted my vacuum cleaner left until last so that I could leave the floors clean but when I turned round it had gone. I had packed an overnight case with a change of clothes to wear on the boat, but that disappeared right under my nose, too. In fact if I took my eyes off anything for a moment it was spirited away.

At one o'clock it was obvious the packing would not be finished in time, so a phone call was made to the shipping office to ask for an extension. It was granted and we were allowed another two hours. Everyone breathed a sigh of relief and welcomed a break for a cup of tea.

Robbie Adam always drove down the Maywick road on his tractor when he went to look at his sheep. We saw him look across at us, then park the tractor by the side of the road and lope across the valley on his long legs to come and wish us goodbye and a safe journey.

'Come back and see us again,' he said, and of course we said we would.

Bobbie Mullay came across too and we took a dram together for friendship's sake.

'This man has to be in Lerwick by four o'clock. You'll have to take him Millie.' 'This' man was a temporary loader, he was also a policeman due to go on duty. It wouldn't do for him to be late.

The Volkswagen was loaded and ready to go. The cats had been bundled into the cat box and put into the van along with Floss. Getting into the driving seat with Michael and the policeman as passengers I drove away from Yawfield for the last time. Setting the policeman down in Lerwick we continued on to the ferry terminal. I checked in at the desk and told them the lorry was on its way. Now all we had to do was sit and wait.

Tap tap tap. I turned my head and saw a smiling, friendly face.

'I have something for you,' she said.

As I followed her to her car I wondered what it could be. From its boot she produced a couple of cardboard boxes. 'A few chickens,' she said. 'The ones that lay green eggs.' I couldn't look at them then, or they might have escaped. I thanked her, I'd long had a hankering after this sort of poultry. No-one really knew what breed they were though the theory was put forward that they came ashore from the Spanish Fleet that was fleeing from Drake. When I opened the back door of the van to put the boxes in the cats were loose. I shoved them back in the box and hoped they'd stay there. It wouldn't be for too long, we should be in Aberdeen at eight in the morning.

We didn't have to wait long before Slim arrived in the Renault van with Pickford's lorry close behind. They reported to the ticket office and very soon we were boarding the ship. First they loaded our animals, then the lorry and then the two vehicles. Floss stayed in the van with the cats, who had once more regained their freedom. When all was secure we went to find our cabins and freshen up.

I was doing my hair and wishing I had a clean blouse to put on when I heard our names being called out on the Tannoy.

'Would Mr and Mrs Vigor please come to the purser's office.'

Whatever's happened now, I thought, as we made our way along the corridor and up the stairs. Alison and Maria were waiting for us.

'Whatever are you two doing here?' I asked.

'We've come to see you off,' they said. 'Only you won't be going.'

'What d'you mean? Why not?' Was this a leg-pull?

'The dockers are on strike in Aberdeen.'

'You're kidding. I don't believe you.' I knew these two. 'Now tell me why you're really here.'

'We brought you a going away present.' Alison gave me a package.

'Thank you. That's nice of you. Can I open it now?'

The package contained a brushed steel tray but what made it special was that the back had been engraved with their names and the date, 1.10.82.

'But you won't be going,' said Alison again.

'You mean it don't you.'

Just then the public address system came to life. 'We're very sorry, ladies and gentlemen, but the *St. Clair* will not be sailing for Aberdeen tonight due to the fact that the dockers are on strike there.' Passengers who were resident in Lerwick and district were requested to return to their homes and to telephone daily for information as to the sailing date. We couldn't do that for we were now literally homeless.

'We told you didn't we,' said Alison and Maria in unison.

The reception area where we stood filled quickly with would-be passengers who were disembarking with their luggage. What were we to do? Maria and Alison said, 'We'll leave you to it,' and they too went down the gangway.

'They can't throw us off with nowhere to go,' said Slim. 'Let's go and find the purser.'

As there were others in a similar position to us we were allowed to stay on board. At least we'd have a roof over our heads until the ship was able to sail.

Lulu, along with Dandy and Rusty, Zoe the goat, Floss the dog, the two cats and six sheep were in the hold, add to them the chickens I had been given and it was a bit like Noah's Ark. Being on the boat for one night would have been no problem but being stuck in Lerwick harbour for an indefinite period was rather different. The shipping company wanted to off-load our animals and put them out to graze but Slim wouldn't allow it. Instead, hay was brought on board for them. The chickens wouldn't survive in cardboard boxes for any length of time. We had no food or water for them or anything to put them in if we had, but it was late, there was nothing to be done until morning.

Next day, Slim and John, Pickford's driver, went to a builder's yard and came back with two tea chests. They had nailed strips of wood to the front of them and turned them into hen coops. We transferred the poultry to them and discovered that we had a cockerel, two hens and three partly grown chickens. From a trailer, parked near the freight shed, we swept up some meal, probably cow cake, that had been spilled and with an empty tin, in which to put water, the poultry were catered for.

We carried hay and buckets of water to the cattle, sheep and the goat. I milked the goat and gave some to the cats and dog. The ship's galley provided scraps to feed them. The cats escaped again and I spent half an hour chasing them round the deck. They played hide and seek under the cattle containers while I crawled on all fours trying to catch them.

Feeding and looking after the animals took only part of the day so I was glad I'd saved my knitting from the clutching hands of the removal men. My knitting pins click clacked during the morning, afternoon and evening and when I was not knitting I went to our cabin and slept. It was a mini holiday for me. No cooking or washing up, no cleaning, no washing, no ironing. I was glad of the rest.

Slim spent most of his time with the lorry driver, a Glasgow man with a dry wit. They spent hours discussing and debating many subjects and lubricating their vocal chords with the contents of many a red can.

Michael toured the ship, played the fruit machines, drank coke and got bored. When after a couple of days the captain announced that the ship would be sailing that night it was indeed welcome news.

People started to re-embark. The atmosphere changed from one of lethargy to that of bustle and work. The ship took on a new lease of life when its engines were started. It shook itself and shuddered. A steady drone and throbbing pulse charged the ship with expectation. I cast aside my knitting, red cans remained on the bar shelf and we went on deck to watch as the *St. Clair* cast off the ties that bound her. Amid shouted orders from the dockers, the rattle of chains and a rumbling surge from her screws, the ferry gradually pulled away from the quay.

We looked down on the upturned faces of the friends and relations of passengers who had come to see them off, spotted Mimie and June among them. Some smiled and waved happily but here and there a hankie was used to wipe away a tear. I waved to Mimie and June, saw Mimie, head bowed, turn and walk away. As the *St. Clair* gathered speed and turned her nose seaward, the figures on the quay grew smaller and smaller until, in the gathering darkness, they were no longer visible.

We went inside then. The journey that had now begun was to bring an end to one period of our lives and be the beginning of another.